BRUSH UP YOUR SPEAKING

by Kim Jong-choon

Topics for Boosting your Speaking Skill

교육과학사

How to use this book

WORD LEVEL

1

WORD LEVEL

주어진 주제에 관한 브레인스토밍을 해서 연관 단어를 적어보세요.

PHRASE LEVEL

1. in the sky
2. fly high
3. call the cabin crew
4. buy a ticket

2

PHRASE LEVEL

위 연관 단어를 기본으로 하여 구(단어+단어)를 적어보세요.

SENTENCE LEVEL

1. An airplane is flying high in the sky.
2. I bought a ticket for New York.

3

SENTENCE LEVEL

위 단어와 구를 활용하여 문장을 적어보세요.

4
Q
질문입니다.

5
POSSIBLE ANSWER I
첫 번째 예시 답안입니다.

6
POSSIBLE ANSWER II
두 번째 예시 답안입니다.

7
WORD BOX
단어 연습 및 뜻풀이입니다.

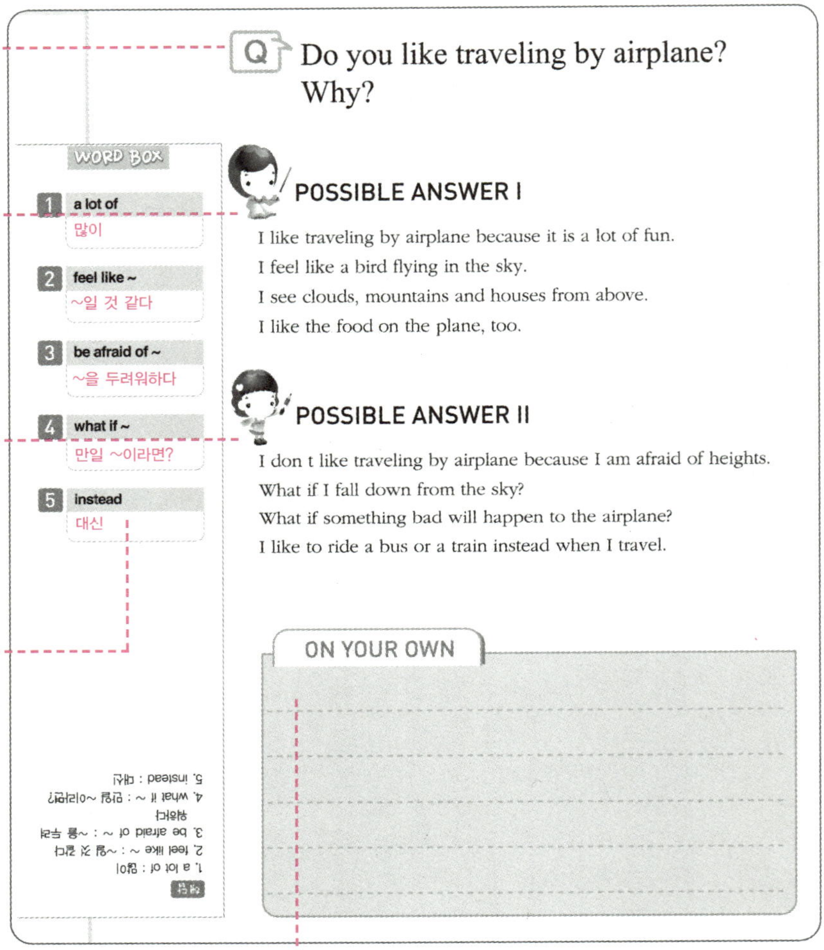
Q Do you like traveling by airplane? Why?

WORD BOX

1 a lot of
많이

2 feel like ~
~일 것 같다

3 be afraid of ~
~을 두려워하다

4 what if ~
만일 ~이라면?

5 instead
대신

정답
1. a lot of : 많이
2. feel like ~ : ~일 것 같다
3. be afraid of ~ : ~을 두려워하다
4. what if ~ : 만일 ~이라면?
5. instead : 대신

POSSIBLE ANSWER I

I like traveling by airplane because it is a lot of fun.
I feel like a bird flying in the sky.
I see clouds, mountains and houses from above.
I like the food on the plane, too.

POSSIBLE ANSWER II

I don t like traveling by airplane because I am afraid of heights.
What if I fall down from the sky?
What if something bad will happen to the airplane?
I like to ride a bus or a train instead when I travel.

ON YOUR OWN

8
ON YOUR OWN
이제 본인의 생각을 글로 적어봅니다.

LISTEN TO THE CD AND FILL IN THE BLANK.

1. I like traveling by airplane because it is a lot of fun.
2. What if I fall down from the sky?
3. I can eat all the food and sometimes ask for more.
4. I like looking at the windows and watching the clouds.

9
LISTEN TO THE CD AND FILL IN THE BLANK.

오디오를 듣고 밑줄을 채워 봅니다.

LISTEN TO THE CD AND WRITE THE SENTENCE.

1. I feel like a bird flying in the sky
2. I like to ride a bus or a train instead was I travel.
3. I like snacks drinks and other food.
4. I like walling inside the plane.

10
LISTEN TO THE CD AND WRITE THE SENTENCE.

오디오를 듣고 전체 문장을 받아 적어 봅니다.

Contents

TOPIC 01

AIRPLANES

WORD LEVEL

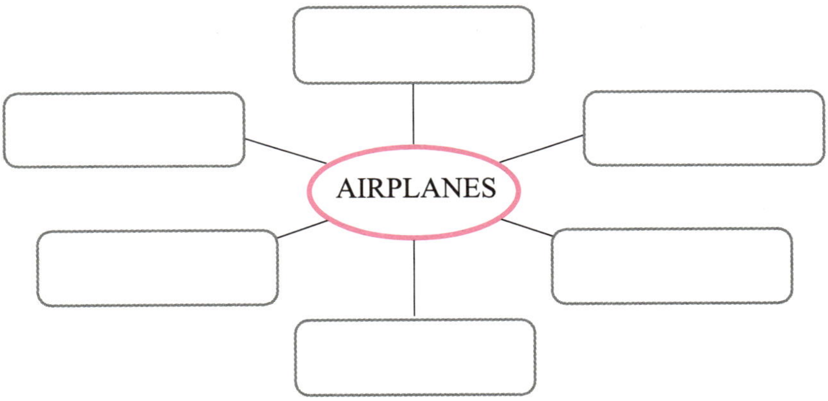

PHRASE LEVEL

1. ____________________

2. ____________________

3. ____________________

4. ____________________

SENTENCE LEVEL

1. ____________________

2. ____________________

1 Question

Q Do you like traveling by airplane? Why?

WORD BOX

1. a lot of
2. feel like ~
3. be afraid of ~
4. what if ~
5. instead

POSSIBLE ANSWER I

I like traveling by airplane because it is a lot of fun.
I feel like a bird flying in the sky.
I see clouds, mountains and houses from above.
I like the food on the plane, too.

POSSIBLE ANSWER II

I don't like traveling by airplane because I am afraid of heights.
What if I fall down from the sky?
What if something bad will happen to the airplane?
I like to ride a bus or a train instead when I travel.

ON YOUR OWN

해답

1. a lot of 많이
2. feel like ~ ~일 것 같다
3. be afraid of ~ ~을 두려워하다
4. what if ~ 만일 ~이라면?
5. instead 대신

2 Question

Q What do you like most when you ride in an airplane?

POSSIBLE ANSWER I

I enjoy the food on the airplane.
I like snacks, drinks and other food.
I can eat all the food and sometimes ask for more.
I can also enjoy some music and watch the latest movies on the plane.

POSSIBLE ANSWER II

I like looking at the windows and watching the clouds.
I like walking inside the plane.
I like watching movies or listening to the radio.
I also like meeting other people.

ON YOUR OWN

WORD BOX

1. serve
2. sometimes
3. delicious
4. ask for
5. walk inside

해답

1. serve 대접하다
2. sometimes 때때로
3. delicious 맛있는
4. ask for 요구하다
5. walk inside 실내를 걷다

Key Expression Practice

LISTEN TO THE CD AND FILL IN THE BLANK.

1. I like traveling by airplane because it is ________ fun.

2. ________ I fall down from the sky?

3. I can eat all the food and sometimes ________ more.

4. I like ________ the windows and watching the clouds.

LISTEN TO THE CD AND WRITE THE SENTENCE.

1. --

2. --

3. --

4. --

TOPIC 02

ANIMALS & PETS

WORD LEVEL

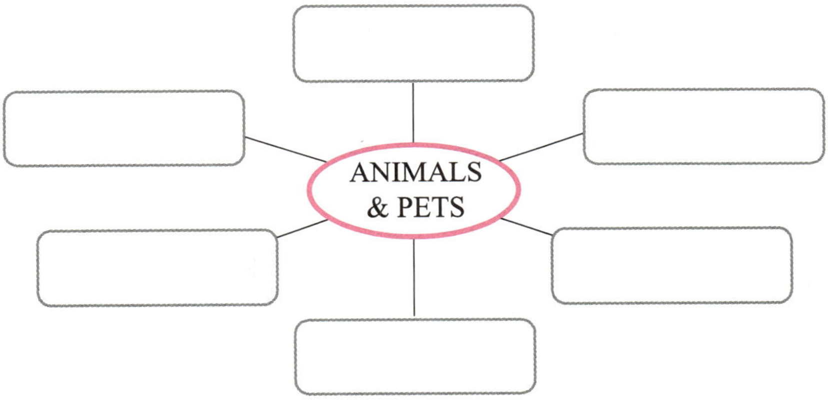

PHRASE LEVEL

1. ______________________ 2. ______________________

3. ______________________ 4. ______________________

SENTENCE LEVEL

1. ____

2. ____

1 Question

Q People love to take care of pets. What can you learn from having a pet?

POSSIBLE ANSWER I

I like having pets. I learn a lot from them.
They are friendly and cheerful all the time.
When I am down, they make me smile and laugh.
My pet is my best friend. I enjoy being with my pet.

POSSIBLE ANSWER II

I don't like to have a pet.
Pets are scary and they might bite me.
My mom doesn't want me to have a pet in the house.
She says it will only destroy her plants and will make the house dirty.

ON YOUR OWN

WORD BOX

1. friendly
2. laugh
3. scary
4. bite
5. destroy

해답

1. friendly 다정한
2. laugh 웃다
3. scary 무서운
4. bite 물다
5. destroy 파괴하다

2 Question

Q If you could be an animal, what kind of animal would you like to be and why?

POSSIBLE ANSWER I

I want to be a lion. Lions are brave as well as strong.
People say they are the king of the jungle.
All the animals are afraid of the lions.
Lions can eat all they want.

POSSIBLE ANSWER II

I want to be an eagle.
I want to fly and go to other places.
Eagles are beautiful birds.
They are very strong.
They can fly high in the sky.

ON YOUR OWN

WORD BOX

1. as well as
2. fly
3. place
4. strong
5. fly high

해답
1. as well as ~도 또한
2. fly 날다
3. place 장소
4. strong 강한
5. fly high 높이 날다

Key Expression Practice

LISTEN TO THE CD AND FILL IN THE BLANK.

1. They are friendly and cheerful ____________ .

2. She says it will only _______ her plants and will make the house dirty.

3. Lions are brave ____________ strong.

4. They can __________ in the sky.

LISTEN TO THE CD AND WRITE THE SENTENCE.

1. --

2. --

3. --

4. --

TOPIC 03

ART

WORD LEVEL

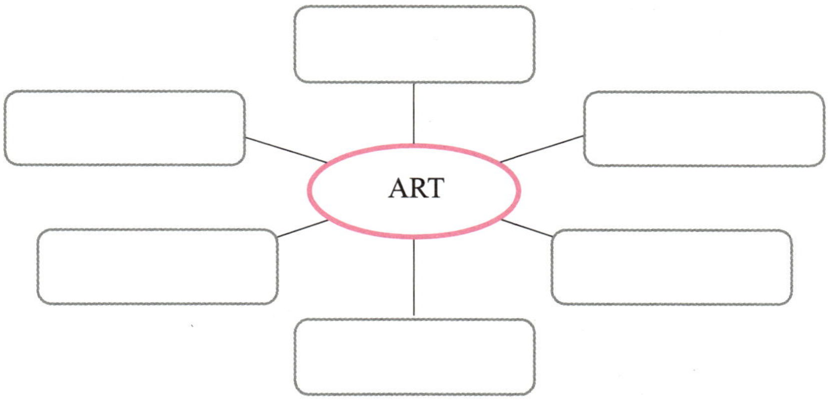

PHRASE LEVEL

1. ______________________ 2. ______________________

3. ______________________ 4. ______________________

SENTENCE LEVEL

1. ____

2. ____

1 Question

Q Students have art classes in school. Do you enjoy art classes? Why?

WORD BOX

1 object

2 forget

3 figure

4 prefer A to B

5 art class

해답
1. object 물체
2. forget 잊어버리다
3. figure 모양, 숫자
4. prefer A to B B보다는 A를 더 선호하다
5. art class 미술 수업

POSSIBLE ANSWER I

I enjoy our art class in school.
We draw and make many objects.
When I draw something, I forget my worries.
I love drawing and thinking.
I want to be a painter someday.

POSSIBLE ANSWER II

I enjoy our art class but I prefer making paper figures to drawing.
Making paper figures is more fun than drawing.
I can make a lot of things like a paper boat, or a paper frog or a paper plane.
I love to play with my paper toys.

ON YOUR OWN

2 Question

Q Do you think cartoons and comics are works of art?

POSSIBLE ANSWER I

I think cartoons and comics are a form of art.
They are colorful and beautiful.
Comics have nice drawings, too.
I like reading comics and watching cartoons.
They are exciting and interesting.

POSSIBLE ANSWER II

I think cartoons and comics are not a form of art.
They are not made by famous painters.
Some cartoons are not good enough to be read.
Some comics have bad drawings and the stories are boring.

ON YOUR OWN

WORD BOX

1 colorful

2 exciting

3 interesting

4 famous

5 enough

정답
1. colorful 색깔이 다양한
2. exciting 신나는
3. interesting 재미있는
4. famous 유명한
5. enough 충분한

Key Expression Practice

LISTEN TO THE CD AND FILL IN THE BLANK.

1. When I ________ something, I forget my worries.

2. I enjoy our art class but I ________ making paper figures to drawing.

3. They are ________ and beautiful.

4. Some cartoons are not good ____________ .

LISTEN TO THE CD AND WRITE THE SENTENCE.

1. --

2. --

3. --

4. --

TOPIC 04

BOOKS

WORD LEVEL

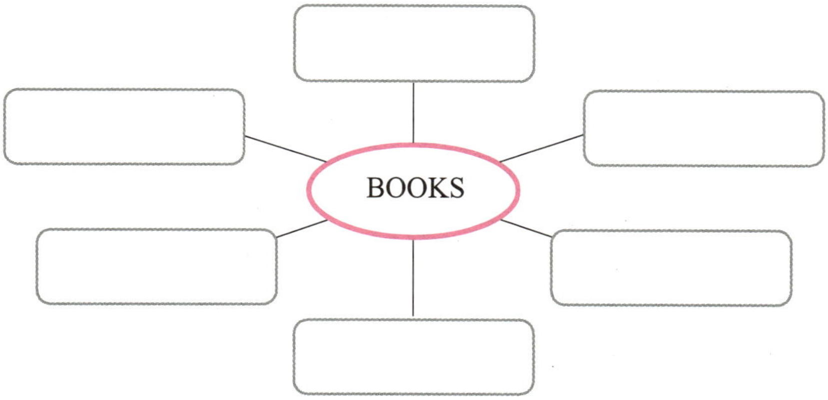

PHRASE LEVEL

1. ____________________ 2. ____________________

3. ____________________ 4. ____________________

SENTENCE LEVEL

1. ____

2. ____

1 Question

Q What was the last book that you have read? What was it all about?

WORD BOX

1 field

2 revolution

3 exciting

4 last

5 history

POSSIBLE ANSWER I

The last book that I read was "Creating Minds".
It was written by Prof. Gardner.
It's about seven great people who are really masters in each field.
The book was fun to read and it was very exciting.

POSSIBLE ANSWER II

The last book that I read was about American history.
I love reading about history.
It was about the American Revolution.
I learned a lot from reading it.

ON YOUR OWN

해답
1. field 영역, 분야
2. revolution 혁명
3. exciting 신나는
4. last 지난, 마지막
5. history 역사

2 Question

Q Do you prefer reading non-fiction books or short fiction stories? Why?

POSSIBLE ANSWER I

I prefer reading non-fiction books than short fiction stories.
They are hard to read but more enjoyable.
Books make you wise if you never give up.
They make you imagine and travel into another world.

POSSIBLE ANSWER II

I prefer reading short fiction stories.
They are easier to read.
If books are difficult to read, I might fall asleep while I am reading.
They even have beautiful pictures in them.
I understand them better thanks to the pictures.

ON YOUR OWN

WORD BOX

1. enjoyable
2. give up
3. imagine
4. fall asleep
5. thanks to

해답

1. enjoyable 즐거운
2. give up 포기하다
3. imagine 상상하다
4. fall asleep 잠에 빠지다
5. thanks to ~의 덕분에

Key Expression Practice

LISTEN TO THE CD AND FILL IN THE BLANK.

1. It's about seven great people who ______________ masters in each field.
2. ________________ that I read was about American History.
3. Books make you wise if you never ____________ .
4. I understand ________________ thanks to the pictures.

LISTEN TO THE CD AND WRITE THE SENTENCE.

1. --
2. --
3. --
4. --

TOPIC 05

BIRTHDAYS

WORD LEVEL

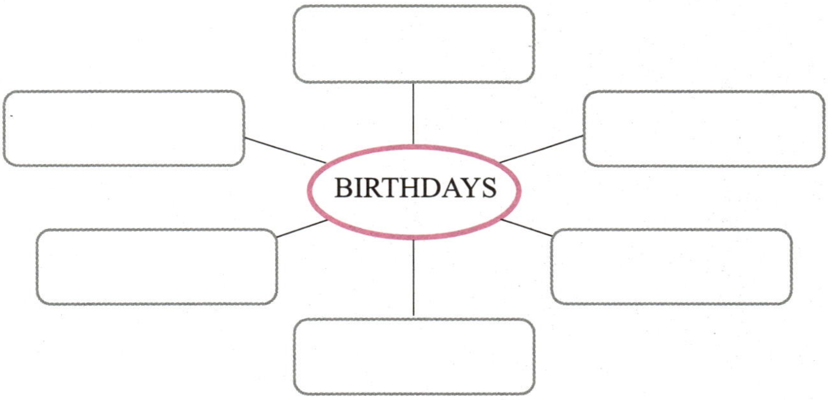

PHRASE LEVEL

1. ______________________ 2. ______________________

3. ______________________ 4. ______________________

SENTENCE LEVEL

1. ____

2. ____

1 Question

Q What gift did you receive on your last birthday?

WORD BOX

1. present
2. worn out
3. electronic dictionary
4. latest
5. feature

해답
1. present 선물
2. worn out 낡은
3. electronic dictionary 전자사전
4. latest 가장 최신의
5. feature 특징

POSSIBLE ANSWER I

I got a soccer ball on my last birthday.
It was a present from my dad.
My old ball was worn out.
My friends and I played soccer with my new ball.

POSSIBLE ANSWER II

My mom gave me an electronic dictionary on my last birthday.
It was the latest model.
It has a lot of cool features.
I use my electronic dictionary when I study in school.

ON YOUR OWN

2 Question

Q What kinds of foods do you usually prepare on your birthday?

POSSIBLE ANSWER I

My mom usually prepares delicious Korean food.
She cooks seaweed soup.
She also cooks fried chicken and hotdogs.
I usually invite all of my friends to my house and have a great time.

POSSIBLE ANSWER II

My mom doesn't cook on my birthday.
She prefers to order food instead.
She orders pizza and buys ice cream and other items that I like.
My friends also enjoy the food that she orders.

ON YOUR OWN

WORD BOX

1 prepare

2 invite

3 usually

4 seaweed soup

5 order

해답
1. prepare 준비하다
2. invite 초청하다
3. usually 보통
4. seaweed soup 미역국
5. order 주문하다

Key Expression Practice

LISTEN TO THE CD AND FILL IN THE BLANK.

1. My old ball was __________ .

2. It was the __________ model.

3. I usually invite all of my friends to my house and __________ .

4. My friends also enjoy the food __________ .

LISTEN TO THE CD AND WRITE THE SENTENCE.

1. --

2. --

3. --

4. --

TOPIC 06

BEAUTY

WORD LEVEL

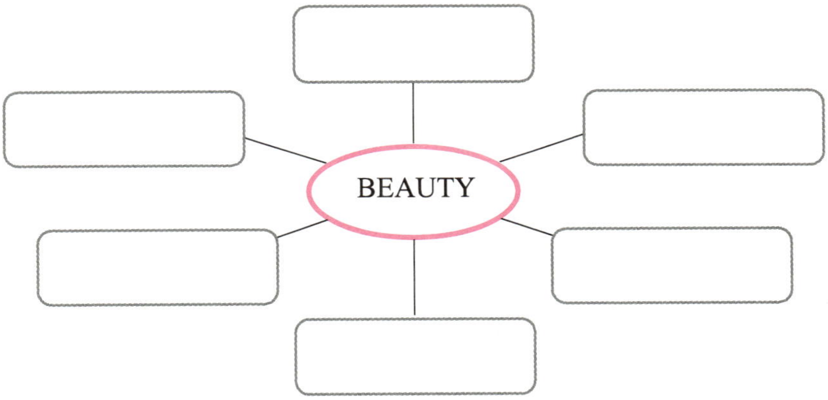

PHRASE LEVEL

1. ____________________ 2. ____________________

3. ____________________ 4. ____________________

SENTENCE LEVEL

1. ____

2. ____

1 Question

Q Who do you think is the most beautiful person alive today?

WORD BOX

1. almost
2. all the time
3. alive
4. smile at
5. sacrifice

POSSIBLE ANSWER I

I think the most beautiful person alive today is my mother.
She always smiles at me.
She sacrifices herself for me and my family.
She prepares almost everything I need.
She kisses me and hugs me all the time.

POSSIBLE ANSWER II

The most beautiful person for me today is Kim Hee-sun.
She is very beautiful.
She is also a very good actress and movie star.
I like her movies and dramas.

ON YOUR OWN

해답
1. almost 거의
2. all the time 항상
3. alive 살아있는
4. smile at ~에게 미소를 짓다
5. sacrifice 희생하다

2 Question

Q Which is more important to you, beauty or intelligence?

POSSIBLE ANSWER I

I think beauty is more important than intelligence.
It is the first thing that you will see.
I like beautiful people.
They look good and kind, too.

POSSIBLE ANSWER II

I think intelligence is more important than beauty.
If you want, you can change your face with plastic surgery.
But you can't add your knowledge easily.
It makes you understand a lot of things.
Intelligence can help you reach your ambition in life.

ON YOUR OWN

WORD BOX

1. the first thing
2. intelligence
3. change
4. plastic surgery
5. ambition

해답

1. the first thing 가장 먼저 할 일
2. intelligence 지식
3. change 바꾸다
4. plastic surgery 성형수술
5. ambition 야망

Key Expression Practice

LISTEN TO THE CD AND FILL IN THE BLANK.

1. She ________________ for me and family.

2. ________________________ for me today is Kim Hee-sun.

3. I think beauty is ____________________ intelligence.

4. Intelligence can help you ____________________ in life.

LISTEN TO THE CD AND WRITE THE SENTENCE.

1. --

2. --

3. --

4. --

TOPIC 07

BEHAVIOR

WORD LEVEL

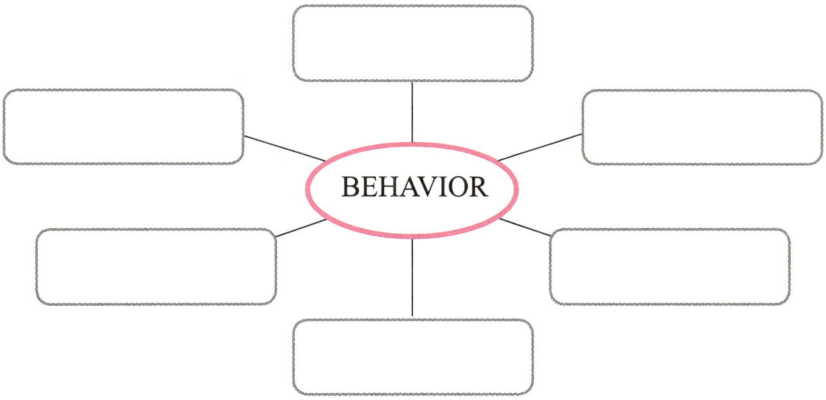

PHRASE LEVEL

1. ______________________ 2. ______________________

3. ______________________ 4. ______________________

SENTENCE LEVEL

1. ____

2. ____

1 Question

Q What is a good behavior to you?

WORD BOX

1. to the end
2. deceive
3. be faithful to
4. no matter what
5. respect

POSSIBLE ANSWER I

Good behavior is when you keep your love to the end.
You never deceive yourself and the person.
You are faithful to the person no matter what happens.
It is because you really love the person.

POSSIBLE ANSWER II

Good behavior is when you help in the house.
You should help the poor and sick people.
You should also respect people who are older than you.
And try to understand others all the time.

ON YOUR OWN

해답

1. to the end 끝까지
2. deceive 속이다
3. be faithful to ~에게 충실하다
4. no matter what 무엇이든지
5. respect 존경하다

2 Question

Q What for you is bad behavior?

POSSIBLE ANSWER I

Bad behavior is when you are deceiving yourself and others.
You copy from your classmates during exams and tests.
You don't follow the rules in school.
You talk back to your teacher.

POSSIBLE ANSWER II

Bad behavior is when you say a bad word to someone.
You hurt other people's feelings.
Sometimes you have fights with classmates.
Othertimes you tell lies to get what you want.

ON YOUR OWN

WORD BOX

1. follow
2. rule
3. talk back
4. hurt
5. have fights

해답

1. follow 따르다
2. rule 규칙
3. talk back 말대꾸하다
4. hurt 상처를 주다
5. have fights 싸우다

Key Expression Practice

LISTEN TO THE CD AND FILL IN THE BLANK.

1. You ________________ the person no matter what happens.

2. You should also ____________________ are older than you.

3. You don't __________________ in school.

4. Sometimes you __________________ classmates.

LISTEN TO THE CD AND WRITE THE SENTENCE.

1. --

2. --

3. --

4. --

TOPIC 08

CELEBRITIES

WORD LEVEL

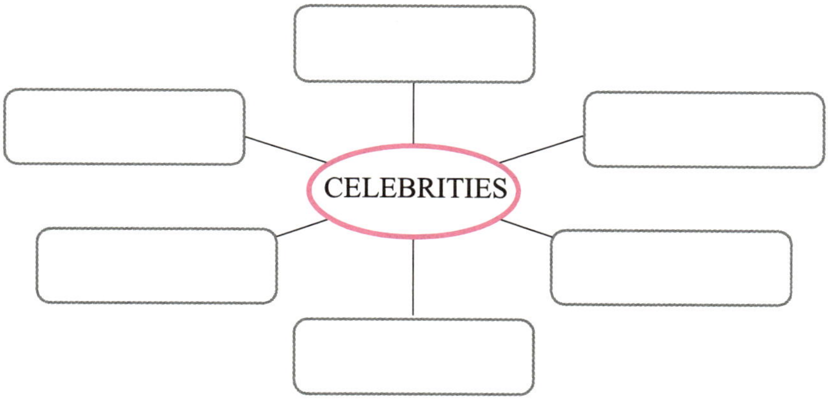

PHRASE LEVEL

1. ______________________ 2. ______________________

3. ______________________ 4. ______________________

SENTENCE LEVEL

1. ____

2. ____

1 Question

Q Have you ever seen a celebrity in person? What did you do?

WORD BOX

1 in person

2 take pictures

3 autograph

4 talent

5 the next day

POSSIBLE ANSWER I

Yes, I have seen a celebrity in person when we were at the mall.
We took pictures with him.
He also signed my notebook with his autograph.
I was so happy.
I showed it to my friends in school the next day.

POSSIBLE ANSWER II

I haven't seen a celebrity in person.
But I always see many on TV.
They look handsome and cool.
They have many talents like dancing, singing and acting.

ON YOUR OWN

해답

1. in person 개인적으로
2. take pictures 사진을 찍다
3. autograph 사인
4. talent 탤런트, 재능
5. the next day 다음 날

2 Question

Q If you could meet one celebrity, who would it be and why?

POSSIBLE ANSWER I

I would like to meet Will Smith.
He is my idol.
He is a very awesome actor.
I love watching his movies.
I want to get his autograph and take pictures with him.

POSSIBLE ANSWER II

I don't like to meet anybody.
I just enjoy watching them on TV.
I think celebrities are just popular people.
They are still people so there's nothing special about them.

ON YOUR OWN

WORD BOX

1 idol

2 awesome

3 popular

4 nothing special

5 anybody

해답
1. idol 우상
2. awesome 멋진
3. popular 인기있는
4. nothing special 특별할 것이 없는
5. anybody 어떤 사람이든지

Key Expression Practice

LISTEN TO THE CD AND FILL IN THE BLANK.

1. Yes, I have seen a celebrity ____________ when we were in the mall.
2. They have many talents like __________ , __________ and __________ .
3. I want to get his autograph and ____________________ him.
4. They are still people so ________________________ about them.

LISTEN TO THE CD AND WRITE THE SENTENCE.

1. --
2. --
3. --
4. --

TOPIC 09

CITIES

WORD LEVEL

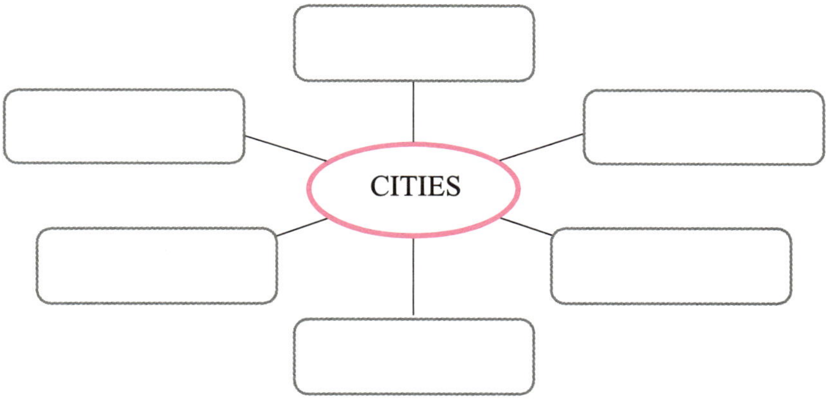

PHRASE LEVEL

1.

2.

3.

4.

SENTENCE LEVEL

1.

2.

1 Question

Q Do you like living in the city? Why?

WORD BOX

1. convenient
2. modern
3. crowded
4. pollution
5. fresher

POSSIBLE ANSWER I

I like living in the city.
It is more convenient.
There are big shops, markets and beautiful parks.
It is also very modern.
I like going to the malls with my friends.

POSSIBLE ANSWER II

I don't like to live in the city.
It is too crowded with people and cars.
There is also a lot of pollution and it is very dirty.
I like to live in the countryside.
The air there is much cleaner and fresher.

ON YOUR OWN

해답
1. convenient 편리한
2. modern 현대적인
3. crowded 사람이 붐비는
4. pollution 공해
5. fresher 더 신선한

2 Question

Q What's your favorite city? Why?

POSSIBLE ANSWER I

My favorite city is Seoul.
It is where I live.
There are many beautiful places to visit here.
It is also very modern.
I like living here because I have many friends and this is where I study.

POSSIBLE ANSWER II

My favorite city is Milan in Italy.
I went there with my family on last vacation.
It was so beautiful.
There are old buildings and big fountains, too.
The food there was also delicious.
I wish I could live in one of the old cities in Europe.

ON YOUR OWN

WORD BOX

1 favorite

2 visit

3 vacation

4 fountain

5 I wish I could

해답
1. favorite 좋아하는
2. visit 방문하다
3. vacation 방학, 휴가
4. fountain 분수
5. I wish I could 내가 할 수만 있다면

Key Expression Practice

LISTEN TO THE CD AND FILL IN THE BLANK.

1. It is more ______________.

2. It ______________________ people and cars.

3. There are ________________________ to visit here.

4. ________________ live in one of the old cities in Europe.

LISTEN TO THE CD AND WRITE THE SENTENCE.

1. --

2. --

3. --

4. --

TOPIC 10 CLASSROOMS

WORD LEVEL

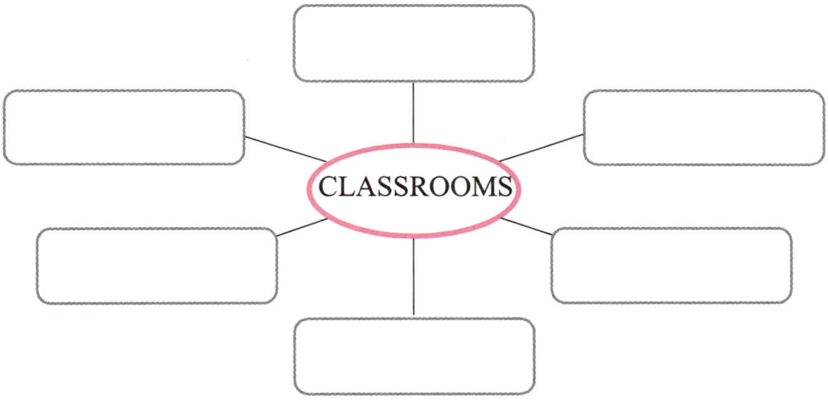

PHRASE LEVEL

1. ______________________ 2. ______________________

3. ______________________ 4. ______________________

SENTENCE LEVEL

1. ____

2. ____

1 Question

Q What do you like in your classroom? Why?

WORD BOX

1. place
2. sticker
3. bulletin board
4. picture
5. design

POSSIBLE ANSWER I

I like my desk in my classroom.
It is my favorite place.
I have all my things in I need in my desk.
I also have beautiful stickers that I put on my desk.

POSSIBLE ANSWER II

I like our bulletin board in our classroom.
It is very colorful.
It has nice pictures on it, too.
I helped my teacher put up those pictures and made some art designs, too.

ON YOUR OWN

해답

1. place 장소
2. sticker 스티커
3. bulletin board 안내판
4. picture 사진
5. design 디자인

2 Question

Q Is your classroom a nice place to study? Why?

POSSIBLE ANSWER I

Our classroom is a nice place to study.
It is very warm and comfortable.
We have a very nice air conditioner in our room.
We have a small library where we can get books to read.

POSSIBLE ANSWER II

Our classroom is not a nice place to study.
It is very hot.
It is also very old and our chairs and desks are old too.
The roof is also leaking and we don't have an air conditioner.

ON YOUR OWN

WORD BOX

1 warm

2 comfortable

3 library

4 old

5 leak

해답
1. warm 따뜻한
2. comfortable 편리한
3. library 도서관
4. old 낡은, 나이가 든
5. leak (물) 새다

Key Expression Practice

LISTEN TO THE CD AND FILL IN THE BLANK.

1. I also have beautiful stickers that I ________ my desk.

2. I ________ my teacher ______ those pictures and ________ some art designs, too.

3. We have a small library where we can ______________ .

4. The roof is also ________ and we don't have an air conditioner.

LISTEN TO THE CD AND WRITE THE SENTENCE.

1. --

2. --

3. --

4. --

TOPIC 11

CLOTHES & FASHION

WORD LEVEL

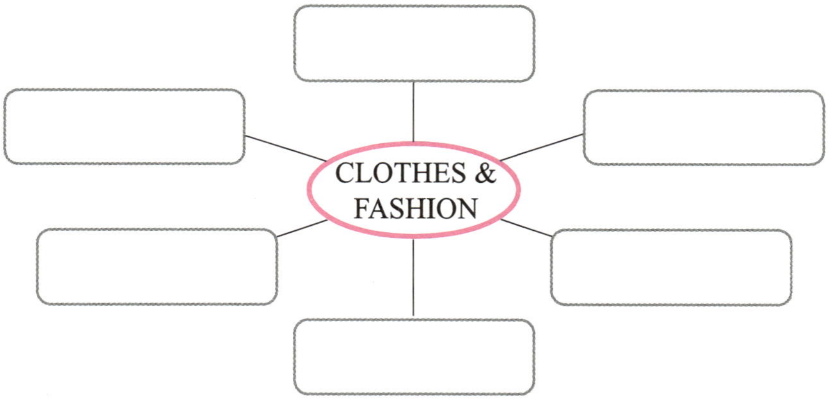

PHRASE LEVEL

1. ______________________ 2. ______________________

3. ______________________ 4. ______________________

SENTENCE LEVEL

1. ____

2. ____

1 Question

Q Would you like to be a fashion model? Why?

POSSIBLE ANSWER I

Yes, I want to be a fashion model.
I want to be famous.
I also like to wear beautiful clothes.
I would like to see myself in magazines.

POSSIBLE ANSWER II

No, I don't want to be a fashion model.
I am shy.
I am afraid to be in front of many people.
I also don't like people looking at me all the time.

WORD BOX

1. famous
2. shy
3. in front of
4. be afraid to
5. look at

해답

1. famous 유명한
2. shy 수줍은
3. in front of ~의 앞에
4. be afraid to 무서워 못하다
5. look at 바라보다

ON YOUR OWN

2 Question

Q What kinds of clothes do you think look good on you?

POSSIBLE ANSWER I

I think a simple shirt, jeans and rubber shoes will look good on me.
I don't like clothes that are too colorful.
I like simple clothes that are comfortable to wear.

POSSIBLE ANSWER II

When I am not wearing my uniform,
I usually wear shorts and short sleeved shirts.
I like wearing slippers when I go out, too.
I feel cool and relaxed.

ON YOUR OWN

WORD BOX

1. simple
2. uniform
3. short sleeved
4. slippers
5. relaxed

해답
1. simple 간단한
2. uniform 유니폼
3. short sleeved 짧은 소매의
4. slippers 슬리퍼
5. relaxed 편안한, 느긋한

Key Expression Practice

LISTEN TO THE CD AND FILL IN THE BLANK.

1. I like to ______________ magazines.
2. I also don't like people ______________ all the time.
3. I think a simple shirt, jeans and rubber shoes will ______________ me.
4. I like wearing slippers ______________ too.

LISTEN TO THE CD AND WRITE THE SENTENCE.

1. --
2. --
3. --
4. --

TOPIC 12

COLORS

WORD LEVEL

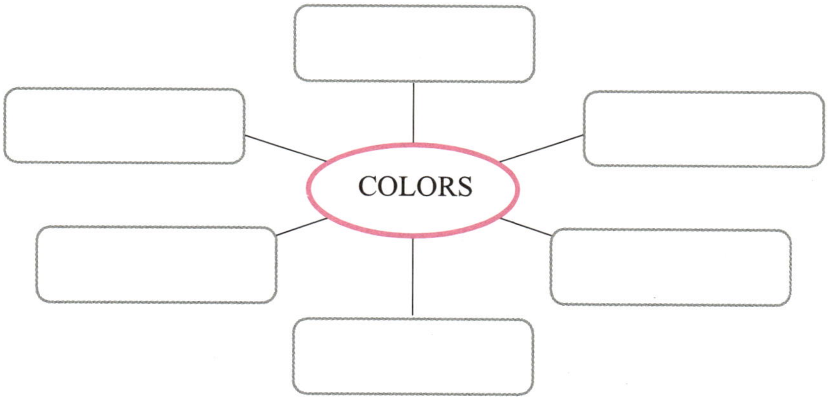

PHRASE LEVEL

1.

2.

3.

4.

SENTENCE LEVEL

1.

2.

1 Question

Q What is your favorite color and why?

WORD BOX

1. match
2. fresh
3. feel better
4. relaxing
5. look cool

POSSIBLE ANSWER I

My favorite color is black.
I like it because it makes me look cool.
I like wearing black clothes.
It also matches well with other colors.

POSSIBLE ANSWER II

Blue is my favorite color.
It looks fresh.
I like looking at the blue sky.
Blue makes me feel better.
It is nice on the eyes and relaxing, too.

ON YOUR OWN

해답

1. match 짝이 되다
2. fresh 신선한
3. feel better 훨씬 기분이 낫다
4. relaxing 편안하게 해주는
5. look cool 멋지게 보이다

2 Question

Q What do you think of people coloring their hair with different colors such as red, blue, green etc.?

POSSIBLE ANSWER I

I think they are so cool!
I like seeing people with colored hair.
When I grow up I would like to color my hair too.
I would like to color my hair orange and blue.

POSSIBLE ANSWER II

I think they look weird.
I don't like seeing people with colored hair.
They look scary.
It makes them look older because of their hair color.

ON YOUR OWN

WORD BOX

1. colored
2. grow up
3. weird
4. scary
5. look older

해답
1. colored 유색의
2. grow up 자라다
3. weird 이상한
4. scary 무서운
5. look older 나이가 더 들어 보인다

Key Expression Practice

LISTEN TO THE CD AND FILL IN THE BLANK.

1. It also ____________________ other colors.

2. It is good to the eyes and ____________ too.

3. __________________ I would like to color my hair, too.

4. It makes them _____________ because of their hair color.

LISTEN TO THE CD AND WRITE THE SENTENCE.

1. --

2. --

3. --

4. --

TOPIC 13

COMICS & COMEDIES

WORD LEVEL

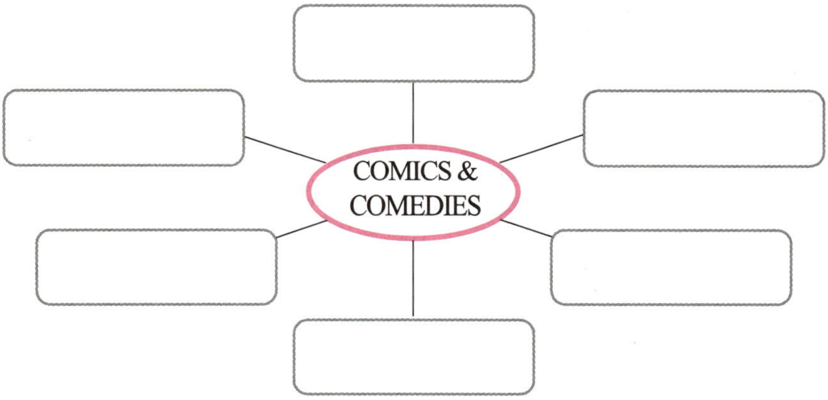

PHRASE LEVEL

1. ____________________ 2. ____________________

3. ____________________ 4. ____________________

SENTENCE LEVEL

1. ____

2. ____

1 Question

Q What kinds of comics do you like and why?

WORD BOX

1 Japanese

2 character

3 amusing

4 understand

5 as well

해답

1. Japanese 일본
2. character 인물, 주인공
3. amusing 흥미로운
4. understand 이해하다
5. as well – 또한

POSSIBLE ANSWER I

I like reading Japanese comics called Manga.
I like reading about my favorite manga character.
The drawings are also very good and amusing.
Sometimes, it is also funny and it makes me laugh.

POSSIBLE ANSWER II

I like reading English comic books.
But I cannot understand all of the words.
So I just look at the pictures.
It has a lot of cool drawings as well.

ON YOUR OWN

2 Question

Q Which program do you like best among the current popular comedies? Why?

POSSIBLE ANSWER I

I think Gag-world is the best one.
I like it because its story is very interesting.
And all the characters are very funny and humorous.
I almost forget my worries when I watch the program.

POSSIBLE ANSWER II

I don't really like any gag program in Korea.
Sometimes I watch some American TV dramas and soap operas.
Because the people in the program speak English,
it helps me to understand their culture and life.

ON YOUR OWN

WORD BOX

1 funny

2 humorous

3 soap opera

4 culture

5 life

해답
1. funny 웃긴
2. humorous 유머스러운
3. soap opera 드라마
4. culture 문화
5. life 삶, 생활

Key Expression Practice

LISTEN TO THE CD AND FILL IN THE BLANK.

1. Sometimes it is also funny and it ________________ .

2. It has a lot of cool drawings __________ .

3. And all the characters are very ________ and ___________ .

4. I ________________ any gag program in Korea.

LISTEN TO THE CD AND WRITE THE SENTENCE.

1. --

2. --

3. --

4. --

TOPIC 14

COMPUTERS & THE INTERNET

WORD LEVEL

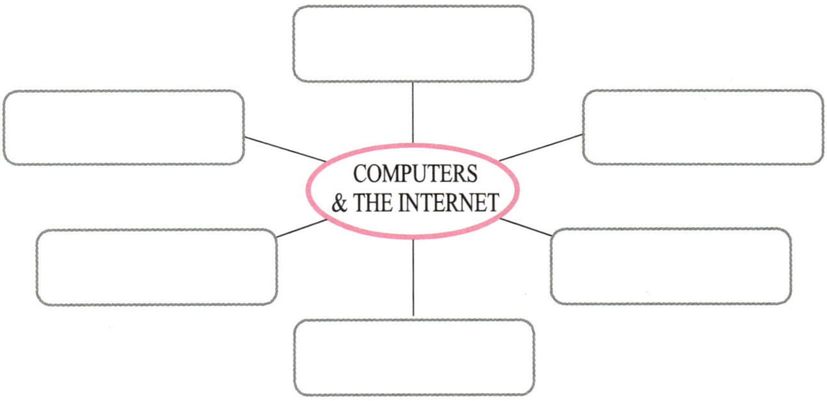

PHRASE LEVEL

1. ______________________ 2. ______________________

3. ______________________ 4. ______________________

SENTENCE LEVEL

1. ____

2. ____

1 Question

Q When do you use your computer?

WORD BOX

1. during the week
2. finish
3. find
4. on weekends
5. upset

POSSIBLE ANSWER I

I use my computer to do my homework.
Using a computer makes my work easier and faster.
I can finish my homework easily.
I can also find a lot of information using my computer.

POSSIBLE ANSWER II

I use my computer when I play computer games.
I like playing computer games with my friends.
But I can only use it on weekends.
My parents will be upset if I play during the week.

ON YOUR OWN

해답

1. during the week 주 동안
2. finish 마치다
3. find 발견하다
4. on weekends 주말에는
5. upset 화가나다

2 Question

Q What do you think is the most serious problem with computers?

POSSIBLE ANSWER I

I think people are addicted to it.
Nowadays, people can t live without a computer.
What if computers disappear one day?
Life will be miserable.

POSSIBLE ANSWER II

People can attack others on the internet.
They write some bad words about others.
They spread bad rumors and speak ill of others.
We should do something else to stop these.

ON YOUR OWN

WORD BOX

1 be addicted to

2 speak ill of

3 disappear

4 miserable

5 attack

해답

1. be addicted to ~에 중독되다
2. speak ill of 나쁘게 말하다
3. disappear 사라지다
4. miserable 비참한
5. attack 공격하다

Key Expression Practice

LISTEN TO THE CD AND FILL IN THE BLANK.

1. Using a computer makes my work ________ and ________.
2. ________________ if I play during the week.
3. I think people ____________ it.
4. They spread bad rumors and __________ others.

LISTEN TO THE CD AND WRITE THE SENTENCE.

1. --
2. --
3. --
4. --

TOPIC 15

DAYS OF THE WEEK

WORD LEVEL

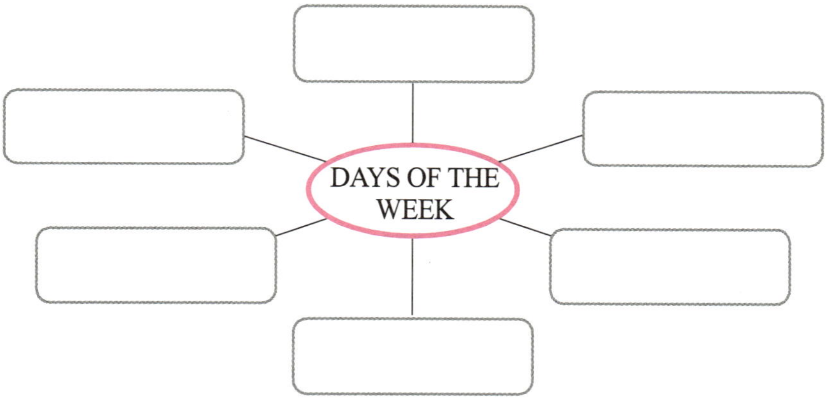

PHRASE LEVEL

1. ______________________ 2. ______________________

3. ______________________ 4. ______________________

SENTENCE LEVEL

1. ____

2. ____

1 Question

Q What is your favorite day of the week? Why?

WORD BOX

1. look forward to
2. don't have to
3. wake up
4. early
5. for myself

POSSIBLE ANSWER I

My favorite day is Friday.
T.G.I.F! (Thank God It's Friday!)
It is the last day of school.
I always look forward to the weekend.
I can play with my friends during the weekend.

POSSIBLE ANSWER II

My favorite day is Saturday.
I don't have to wake up early or go to school.
I have the whole day for myself.
I can play with my friends or watch TV.

ON YOUR OWN

해답

1. look forward to
–를 간절히 고대하다
2. don't have to
–할 필요가 없다
3. wake up 깨어나다
4. early 이른, 일찍이
5. for myself 나 자신을 위해서

2 Question

Q What day of the week do you least like and why?

POSSIBLE ANSWER I

I don't like Mondays.
Blue Monday!
I have to wake up early and prepare for school.
I always feel tired on Mondays.
I sometimes, go to school late on Mondays.

POSSIBLE ANSWER II

I don't like Fridays.
We always have tests on Fridays.
We also have to clean our room, too.
Sometimes, we also have practical tests in PE class.

ON YOUR OWN

WORD BOX

1. Blue Monday
2. prepare for
3. feel tired
4. practical
5. PE class

해답

1. Blue Monday 우울한 월요일
2. prepare for ~를 준비하다
3. feel tired 피곤하다
4. practical 실질적인
5. PE class 체육 수업

Key Expression Practice

LISTEN TO THE CD AND FILL IN THE BLANK.

1. It is ____________________ .

2. I don't have to ________________ or go to school.

3. I sometimes go to school ________________ .

4. Sometimes we also ____________________ in PE class.

LISTEN TO THE CD AND WRITE THE SENTENCE.

1. --

2. --

3. --

4. --

TOPIC 16

DREAMS

WORD LEVEL

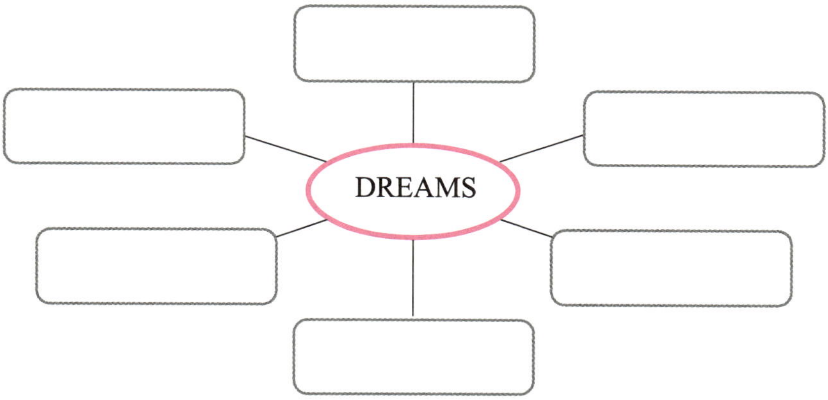

PHRASE LEVEL

1. ______________________ 2. ______________________

3. ______________________ 4. ______________________

SENTENCE LEVEL

1. ____

2. ____

1 Question

Q What is the nicest dream that you can remember?

WORD BOX

1. planet
2. astronaut
3. name after
4. discover
5. different

POSSIBLE ANSWER I

The nicest dream that I had was going to another planet.
In my dream, I became an astronaut.
I visited another planet.
I discovered the planet, so it was named after me.

POSSIBLE ANSWER II

I dreamed that I was a bird.
I was flying in the sky.
I felt the cool wind on my face.
I was able to go to different places.
Everything was so small from the sky and it felt great to fly.

ON YOUR OWN

해답
1. planet 행성
2. astronaut 우주비행사
3. name after ~의 이름을 따서 짓다
4. discover 발견하다
5. different 다른

2 Question

Q Do you believe that dreams can sometimes predict the future? Why?

POSSIBLE ANSWER I

Yes, I do.
I think dreams can tell us about our future.
We may know what will happen to us by our dreams.
Dreams can be signs of things to come.
They can show us some bad things in advance.

POSSIBLE ANSWER II

I don't believe that dreams can predict the future.
We dream of something because we think about it all the time.
Sometimes our dreams are just part of our imagination.
We should not look at it as a sign for telling what will happen in the future.

ON YOUR OWN

WORD BOX

1. future
2. happen
3. in advance
4. predict
5. imagination

해답

1. future 미래
2. happen 발생하다
3. in advance 미리, 사전에
4. predict 예견하다
5. imagination 상상

Key Expression Practice

LISTEN TO THE CD AND FILL IN THE BLANK.

1. I discovered the planet so it was ______________ me.

2. Everything was so small from the sky and ________________ .

3. I think dreams can ______________________ .

4. We should not look at it as a sign for telling ___________________ in the future.

LISTEN TO THE CD AND WRITE THE SENTENCE.

1. --

2. --

3. --

4. --

TOPIC 17

DISLIKES & LIKES

WORD LEVEL

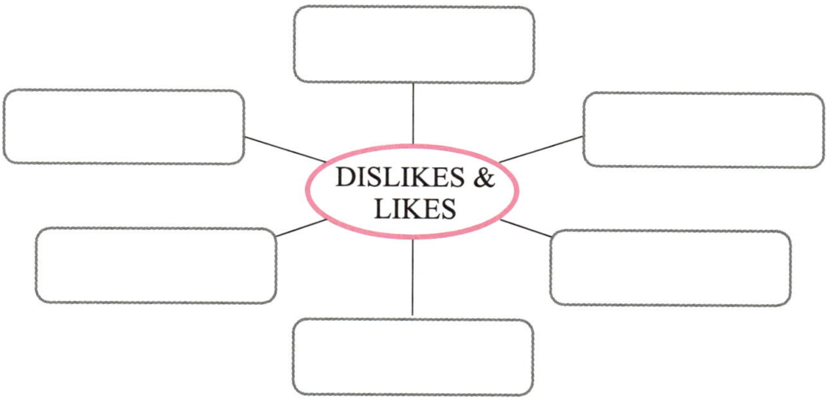

PHRASE LEVEL

1. ______________________ 2. ______________________

3. ______________________ 4. ______________________

SENTENCE LEVEL

1. ____

2. ____

1 Question

Q What kinds of books do you like to read?

POSSIBLE ANSWER I

I like reading history books.

I like reading about important events in history.

It is like traveling through time.

I learn a lot from reading history books.

POSSIBLE ANSWER II

I like reading comic books.

It is more entertaining because it has cool pictures.

I like reading and looking at the drawings.

I have a big comic book collection.

ON YOUR OWN

WORD BOX

1 important

2 event

3 travel

4 entertaining

5 collection

해답

1. important 중요한
2. event 사건
3. travel 여행하다
4. entertaining 재미있는
5. collection 수집

2 Question

Q Do you like watching foreign films? Why or why not?

POSSIBLE ANSWER I

Yes, I like watching foreign films.
I learn a lot about another country's culture.
I also familiarize myself with their language.
I can improve my listening skills when I watch foreign films.

POSSIBLE ANSWER II

I don't like watching foreign films.
I find it hard to understand.
I prefer to watch Korean films.
I watch movies in order to enjoy myself.

ON YOUR OWN

WORD BOX

1. familiarize
2. language
3. improve
4. film
5. enjoy

해답

1. familiarize 익숙시키다
2. language 언어
3. improve 향상시키다
4. film 영화
5. enjoy 즐기다

Key Expression Practice

LISTEN TO THE CD AND FILL IN THE BLANK.

1. I like reading about ______________________ .
2. It is ________________ because it has cool pictures.
3. I also ____________________ their language.
4. I watch movies ___________ enjoy myself.

LISTEN TO THE CD AND WRITE THE SENTENCE.

1. --
2. --
3. --
4. --

TOPIC 18

DESCRIBING SOMETHING

WORD LEVEL

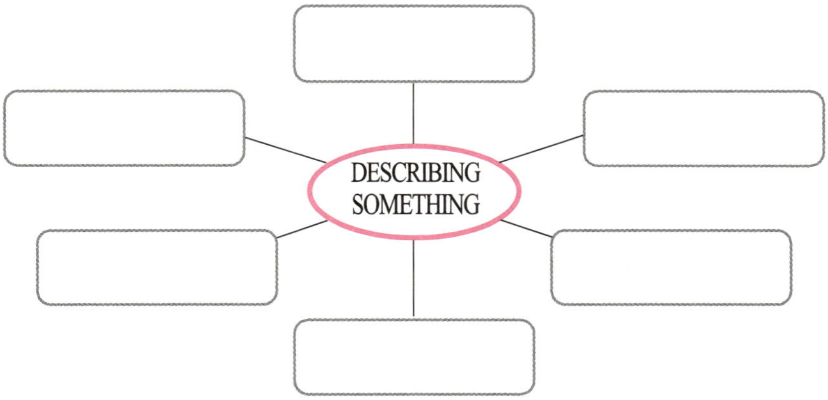

PHRASE LEVEL

1. ______________________ 2. ______________________

3. ______________________ 4. ______________________

SENTENCE LEVEL

1. ____

2. ____

1 Question

Q Describe your room. What does it look like?

WORD BOX

1 share

2 double deck bed

3 sleep

4 own

5 study table

POSSIBLE ANSWER I

My room is not big.
I share my room with my brother.
We sleep in a double deck bed.
We have a study table and a bathroom.

POSSIBLE ANSWER II

My room is big.
I have my room on my own.
I have a big bed and a study table.
I also have my own bathroom.

ON YOUR OWN

해답

1. share 나누다
2. double deck bed 이층침대
3. sleep 잠자다
4. own 스스로의
5. study table 책상

2 Question

Q Describe your best friend. What does he or she look like?

POSSIBLE ANSWER I

My best friend is a tall boy.
He doesn't wear glasses and he has short hair.
He likes to play basketball.
He teaches me how to play basketball, too.

POSSIBLE ANSWER II

My best friend is very pretty.
She has big eyes and a long, curly hair.
She is also taller than me.
She likes eating chocolates and chips.

ON YOUR OWN

WORD BOX

1. wear
2. short
3. pretty
4. curly
5. chips

해답

1. wear 입다
2. short 짧은
3. pretty 예쁜
4. curly 곱슬머리의
5. chips 칩

Key Expression Practice

LISTEN TO THE CD AND FILL IN THE BLANK.

1. We sleep ______________________ .

2. I have my room ______________ .

3. He teaches me __________ play basketball, too.

4. She has ___________ and a ______________ hair.

LISTEN TO THE CD AND WRITE THE SENTENCE.

1. --

2. --

3. --

4. --

TOPIC 19

FAMILY

WORD LEVEL

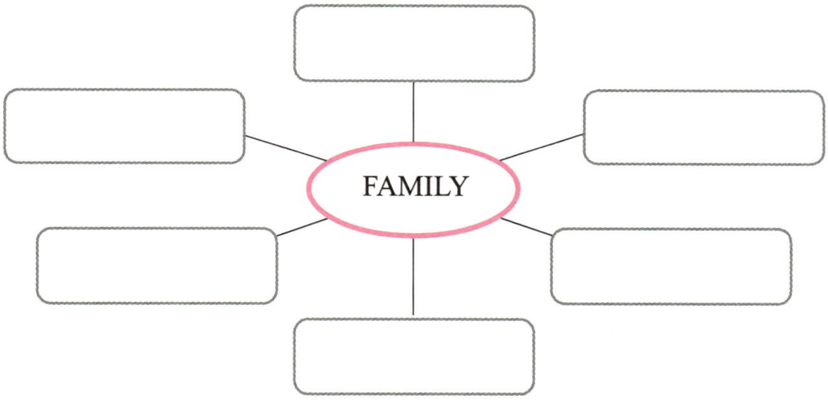

PHRASE LEVEL

1. ____________________ 2. ____________________

3. ____________________ 4. ____________________

SENTENCE LEVEL

1. ____

2. ____

1 Question

Q Do you have to clean your own room? Why?

WORD BOX

1. check
2. scold
3. concentrate on
4. do the cleaning
5. too ~ to -

해답
1. check 확인하다
2. scold 꾸짖다
3. concentrate on 집중하다
4. do the cleaning 청소를 하다
5. too ~ to - 너무 ~해서 -못하다

POSSIBLE ANSWER I

Yes, I have to clean my room.
My mom will get angry if I don't clean my room.
She usually checks my room every time.
She will scold me if it is dirty.
I have to keep my dirty clothes in one place.

POSSIBLE ANSWER II

I don't clean my room.
My mom does it for me.
She says that I have to concentrate on my studies.
So she does the cleaning.
We also have a helper if my mom is too busy to clean my room.

ON YOUR OWN

2 Question

Q What does your father do? What's his job?

POSSIBLE ANSWER I

My father is a police officer.
He works for our society.
He works from morning until night.
When I grow up, I also want to be a police officer just like my father.

POSSIBLE ANSWER II

My father is a businessman.
He has his own company.
He has a big office.
I sometimes go there and stay in his office when he has meetings.
He works in a very tall building with lots of people.

ON YOUR OWN

WORD BOX

1. society
2. from morning till night
3. company
4. stay
5. lots of

해답

1. society 사회
2. from morning till night 아침부터 밤까지
3. company 회사
4. stay 지내다
5. lots of 많은

Key Expression Practice

LISTEN TO THE CD AND FILL IN THE BLANK.

1. My mom will ____________ if I don't clean my room.

2. We also have a helper if my mom is ________________ my room.

3. He works ______________________ .

4. I sometimes go there and stay in his office ____________________ .

LISTEN TO THE CD AND WRITE THE SENTENCE.

1. --

2. --

3. --

4. --

TOPIC 20

FAVORITES

WORD LEVEL

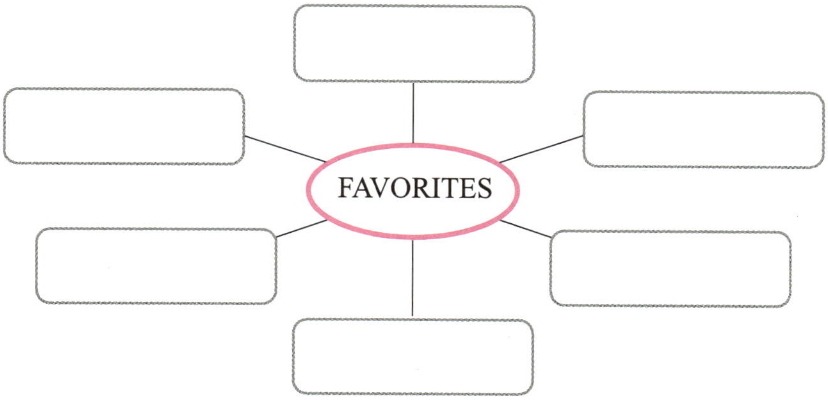

PHRASE LEVEL

1. ______________________ 2. ______________________

3. ______________________ 4. ______________________

SENTENCE LEVEL

1. ____

2. ____

1 Question

Q What is your favorite food and why?

WORD BOX

1. be worried about
2. edible
3. in particular
4. picky
5. as long as

해답

1. be worried about 걱정을 하다
2. edible 먹을 수 있는
3. in particular 특별히
4. picky 까다로운
5. as long as ~하는 한

POSSIBLE ANSWER I

My favorite food is spaghetti.
It is very delicious.
I also like pizza and hamburgers.
I love eating all of it.
My mom is worried about me because I eat too much fast food.

POSSIBLE ANSWER II

I don't have any favorite food in particular.
I just eat all kinds of food.
I am not very picky with the food that I eat.
As long as it is edible, I will eat it.

ON YOUR OWN

2 Question

Q What is your favorite subject in school?

POSSIBLE ANSWER I

My favorite subject is English.
English is a very interesting subject.
I like learning new words and using them in talking to my friends.
It is so much fun to learn English.

POSSIBLE ANSWER II

I like math.
Some people find it hard to learn math.
But I am very comfortable with it.
I think it is because I started math studying in my childhood.

ON YOUR OWN

WORD BOX

1. subject
2. learn
3. be comfortable with
4. start
5. in my childhood

해답

1. subject 과목
2. learn 배우다
3. be comfortable with 편해하다
4. start 시작하다
5. in my childhood 나의 어린시절에

Key Expression Practice

LISTEN TO THE CD AND FILL IN THE BLANK.

1. My mom ________________ me because I eat too much fast food.
2. I am not ________________ the food that I eat.
3. English is ________________________ .
4. But I ________________________ it.

LISTEN TO THE CD AND WRITE THE SENTENCE.

1. --
2. --
3. --
4. --

TOPIC 21

FOODS & EATING

WORD LEVEL

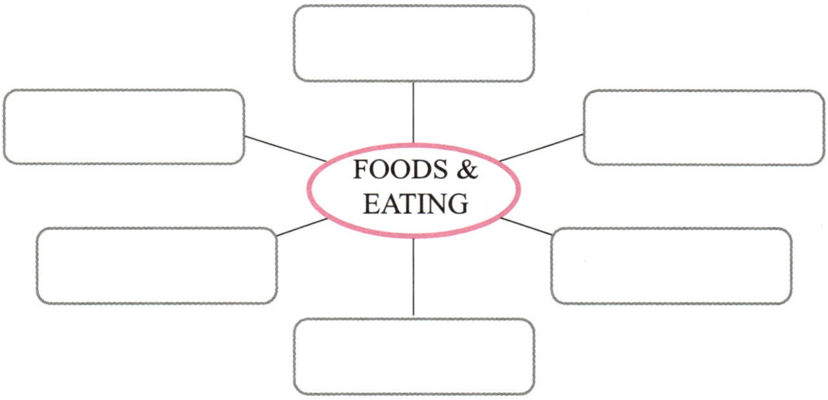

PHRASE LEVEL

1. ______________________ 2. ______________________

3. ______________________ 4. ______________________

SENTENCE LEVEL

1. ____

2. ____

1 Question

Q Do you like to eat a lot of food everyday? Why?

WORD BOX

1 throughout the day

2 fat

3 carry out

4 That's why

5 get hungry

해답

1. throughout the day 하루 종일
2. fat 뚱뚱한
3. carry out 실행하다
4. That's why 그것이 이유이다
5. get hungry 배가 고프다

POSSIBLE ANSWER I

Yes, I like eating a lot.
Eating keeps me strong throughout the day.
It gives me the energy to carry out a lot of things.

POSSIBLE ANSWER II

No, I don't like eating a lot.
I don't want to be fat.
I have a classmate in school and he eats a lot.
That's why he is very fat.
I just eat enough so that I don't get hungry.

ON YOUR OWN

2 Question

Q Do you like eating fruits? Why?

POSSIBLE ANSWER I

Yes, I like eating fruits.
Fruits are very delicious and nutritious.
It makes our body healthy.
I like all kinds of fruits especially mangoes, pineapples and grapes.

POSSIBLE ANSWER II

I like fruits but not all of them.
Some fruits have a weird taste.
I don't like the smell.
I only eat apples and oranges.
I don't like eating durian or peaches.

ON YOUR OWN

WORD BOX

1. nutritious
2. healthy
3. especially
4. smell
5. durian

해답
1. nutritious 영양분 있는
2. healthy 건강한
3. especially 특별하게
4. smell 냄새 맡다
5. durian 두리안(열대과일)

Key Expression Practice

LISTEN TO THE CD AND FILL IN THE BLANK.

1. It gives me the energy to ______________ a lot of things.

2. ______________ he is very fat.

3. Fruits are very ______________ and ______________ .

4. Some fruits have ______________ .

LISTEN TO THE CD AND WRITE THE SENTENCE.

1. ____

2. ____

3. ____

4. ____

TOPIC 22

FRIENDS

WORD LEVEL

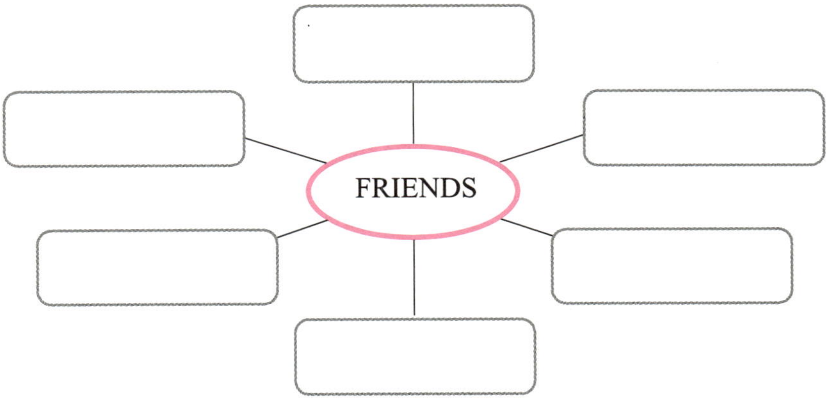

PHRASE LEVEL

1. ______________________ 2. ______________________

3. ______________________ 4. ______________________

SENTENCE LEVEL

1. ____

2. ____

1 Question

Q How do you make friends with someone?

WORD BOX

1. ask questions
2. talk about
3. kindness
4. ask if
5. get to know

해답

1. ask questions 질문을 하다
2. talk about ~에 대하여 말하다
3. kindness 친절
4. ask if ~인지 물어보다
5. get to know 알게 되다

POSSIBLE ANSWER I

Well, I usually talk to him or her.
I also introduce myself.
I ask questions about him/her.
We talk about the things that we like to do.
We also talk about the things that we enjoy doing.

POSSIBLE ANSWER II

I just try to be nice to the person.
I show my kindness to the person.
I ask if I can help the person first.
By helping the person, I can get to know the person.

ON YOUR OWN

2 Question

Q What activities do you do with your best friend?

POSSIBLE ANSWER I

My best friend and I love playing soccer.
We play soccer all the time.
He is very good at soccer.
Sometimes, he teaches me some moves.

POSSIBLE ANSWER II

My best friend and I have different preferences.
I like playing chess while he likes playing basketball.
So we learn from each other.
I teach him how to play chess and he teaches me how to play basketball.

ON YOUR OWN

WORD BOX

1. all the time
2. be good at
3. preference
4. each other
5. sometimes

해답
1. all the time 항상
2. be good at ~를 잘하다
3. preference 선호
4. each other 서로서로
5. sometimes 때때로

Key Expression Practice

LISTEN TO THE CD AND FILL IN THE BLANK.

1. We ________________ that we like to do.

2. By helping the person, I can ________________ .

3. ____________ he teaches me some moves.

4. My best friend and I have ________________ .

LISTEN TO THE CD AND WRITE THE SENTENCE.

1. --

2. --

3. --

4. --

TOPIC 23

FREE TIME

WORD LEVEL

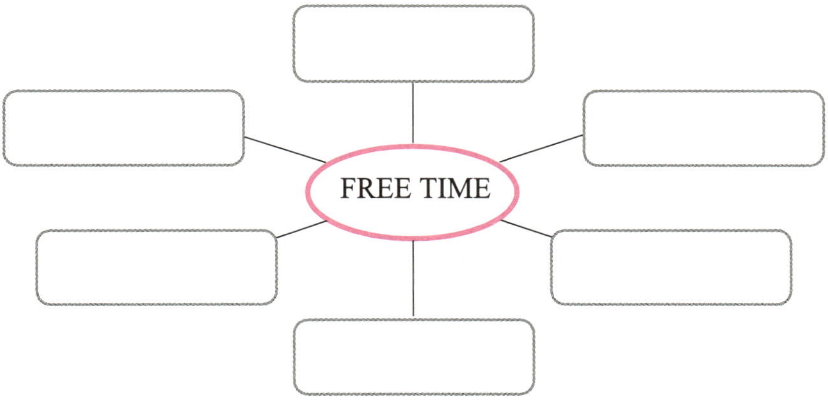

PHRASE LEVEL

1. ______________________ 2. ______________________

3. ______________________ 4. ______________________

SENTENCE LEVEL

1. ____

2. ____

1 Question

Q What do you do during your free time?

WORD BOX

1. free time
2. sleep late
3. get some sleep
4. listen to music
5. play soccer with

POSSIBLE ANSWER I

I like playing video games.
I play video games during my free time.
Sometimes I also play basketball.
I also play soccer with my friends.
I like being with my friends during my free time.

POSSIBLE ANSWER II

I like sleeping during my free time.
I study everyday and sleep late.
So when I have free time, I get some sleep.
I also like listening to music.

ON YOUR OWN

해답

1. free time 자유시간
2. sleep late 늦게 자다
3. get some sleep 잠을 취하다
4. listen to music 음악을 듣다
5. play soccer with –와 축구를 하다

2 Question

Q Which do you prefer, watching TV or internet surfing?

POSSIBLE ANSWER I

I prefer watching TV.
I like watching my favorite TV shows.
I usually can't watch TV during the week.
I can only watch TV on weekends so I spend the weekends watching TV.

POSSIBLE ANSWER II

I like internet surfing more than watching TV.
Internet surfing is more fun and exciting than watching TV.
Some TV shows are not realistic.
So I would rather surf on the internet.

ON YOUR OWN

WORD BOX

1 spend

2 internet surfing

3 usually

4 more fun

5 realistic

해답
1. spend 소비하다
2. internet surfing 인터넷 서핑
3. usually 보통
4. more fun 더욱 재미있는
5. realistic 현실적인

Key Expression Practice

LISTEN TO THE CD AND FILL IN THE BLANK.

1. I like being with my friends ______________________ .

2. So when I have free time, I __________________ .

3. I can only watch TV on weekends so I __________ the weekends _____________ TV.

4. Internet surfing is ________________________ than watching TV.

LISTEN TO THE CD AND WRITE THE SENTENCE.

1. --

2. --

3. --

4. --

TOPIC 24

GOALS

WORD LEVEL

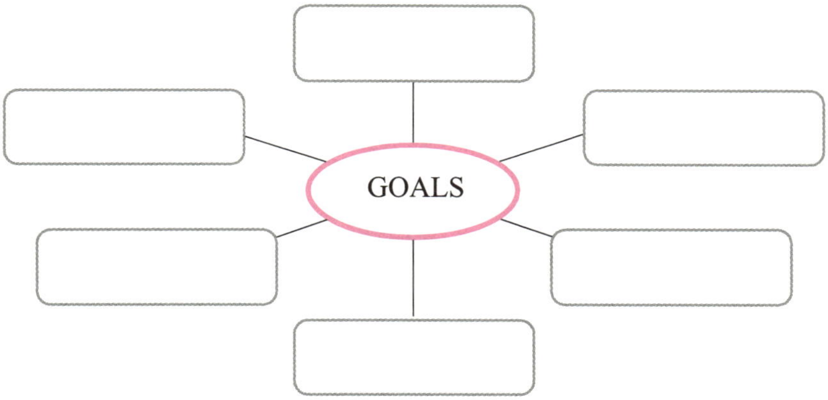

PHRASE LEVEL

1. ______________________ 2. ______________________

3. ______________________ 4. ______________________

SENTENCE LEVEL

1. ____

2. ____

1 Question

Q What is your goal in life when you grow up?

WORD BOX

1. grow up
2. fly a plane
3. sick
4. hospital
5. heal

POSSIBLE ANSWER I

I want to be a pilot when I grow up.
I love to fly.
I want to fly a plane just like the ones I see on TV.
I think it is very cool and exciting.

POSSIBLE ANSWER II

I want to be a doctor when I grow up.
I want to help a lot of sick and poor people.
I want to have my own hospital.
I want to go to Africa to heal the sick people there.

ON YOUR OWN

해답

1. grow up 자라다
2. fly a plane 비행기를 운행하다
3. sick 아픈
4. hospital 병원
5. heal 치료하다

2 Question

Q How important are goals to you?

POSSIBLE ANSWER I

Goals are very important to me.
My goals help me to get all the things that I want.
If I want a new MP3 player, I have to save a lot of money so I can buy it.
To set goals is the first step to achieve them.

POSSIBLE ANSWER II

Goals are not that important to me.
Some goals are hard to reach.
Sometimes goals don't happen.
Most people who have goals do not accomplish them anyway.
It is better to let things happen themselves.

ON YOUR OWN

WORD BOX

1. save
2. achieve
3. anyway
4. accomplish
5. let

해답

1. save 아끼다, 저축하다
2. achieve 성취하다
3. anyway 어쨌든
4. accomplish 성취하다
5. let 시키다

Key Expression Practice

LISTEN TO THE CD AND FILL IN THE BLANK.

1. I want to ______________ just like the ones I see on TV.

2. I want to help ______________________________ .

3. To set goals is __________________________ them.

4. Most people __________________ do not accomplish them anyway.

LISTEN TO THE CD AND WRITE THE SENTENCE.

1. --

2. --

3. --

4. --

TOPIC 25

GIFTS

WORD LEVEL

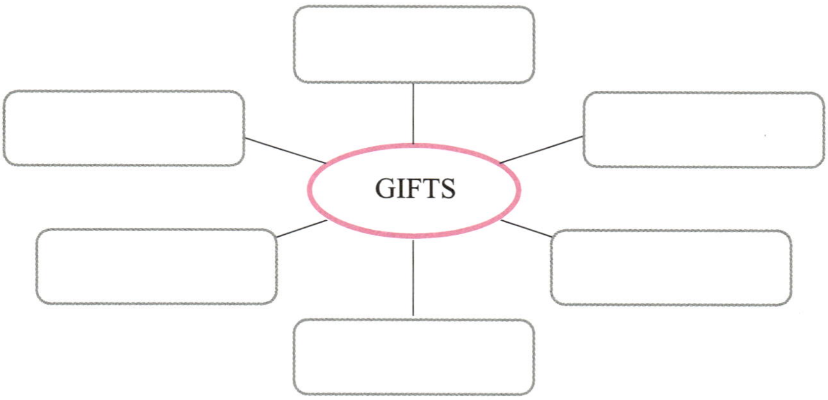

PHRASE LEVEL

1.

2.

3.

4.

SENTENCE LEVEL

1.

2.

1 Question

Q What gift would you want to receive on your birthday?

WORD BOX

1 feature

2 on its own

3 turn off

4 old fashioned

5 wonderful

해답
1. feature 특징
2. on its own 스스로
3. turn off 끄다
4. old fashioned 낡은 방식의
5. wonderful 훌륭한

POSSIBLE ANSWER I

I would want to have a new electronic dictionary for my birthday.
My electronic dictionary is very old.
Sometimes, it turns off on its own.
I want a new model that has many new features.

POSSIBLE ANSWER II

I want to have a new cell phone on my birthday.
My cell phone is very old fashioned.
All of my friends have a smart phone.
It would be wonderful if I can find some information on my phone.

ON YOUR OWN

2 Question

Q What gift will you give to your mom on her birthday?

POSSIBLE ANSWER I

I would like to buy a new red jacket for my mom.
I think it will look good on her.
The jacket that she is using is very old.
My mom saves money for us,
so I am willing to buy a fancy gift for her.

POSSIBLE ANSWER II

I want to give my mom a cook book.
My mom loves to cook.
She likes learning new dishes.
I am sure she will like a cook book.

ON YOUR OWN

WORD BOX

1. would like to
2. jacket
3. be willing to
4. dishes
5. be sure

해답

1. would like to -하고 싶다
2. jacket 재킷
3. be willing to -할 의지가 있다
4. dishes 요리
5. be sure 확실하게

Key Expression Practice

LISTEN TO THE CD AND FILL IN THE BLANK.

1. I want a new model that has ____________________ .

2. ____________________ if I can find some information on the phone.

3. My mom saves money for us, so ____________ buy a fancy gift for her.

4. ____________ she will like a cook book.

LISTEN TO THE CD AND WRITE THE SENTENCE.

1. --

2. --

3. --

4. --

TOPIC 26

GREAT INVENTIONS

WORD LEVEL

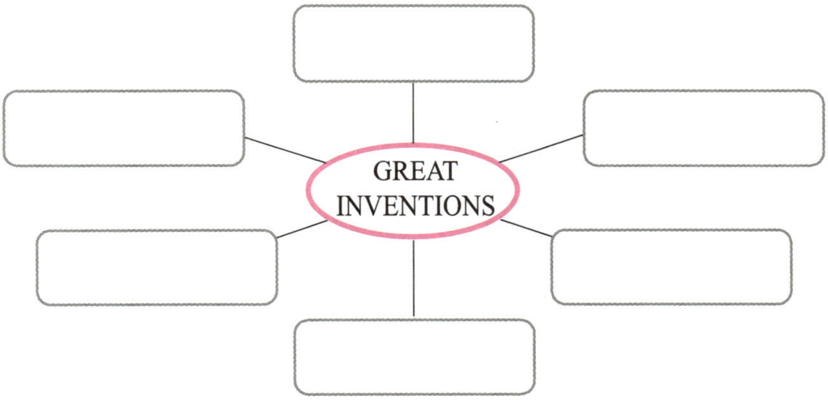

PHRASE LEVEL

1.

2.

3.

4.

SENTENCE LEVEL

1.

2.

1 Question

Q If you could invent anything, what would it be and why?

WORD BOX

1. invent
2. nutrient
3. don't need to
4. for a long time
5. no longer

POSSIBLE ANSWER I

I want to invent a food pill.
It will be a capsule that you just need to eat once.
It will have all the nutrients that you need for the day.
It will also be handy because you can take it anywhere.

POSSIBLE ANSWER II

I want to invent a teleport machine.
People can go to another place faster.
They don't need to take the plane or the train.
They no longer have to travel for a long time.

ON YOUR OWN

해답

1. invent 발명하다
2. nutrient 영양가가 있는
3. don't need to 할 필요가 없다
4. for a long time 한참 동안
5. no longer 더 이상 ~아니다

2 Question

Q What do you think is the greatest invention ever made? Why?

POSSIBLE ANSWER I

I think the best invention ever made was the telephone.
We can talk with other people even if they are in another place.
It helped a lot with communication.
It made people nearer and happier.

POSSIBLE ANSWER II

I think the greatest invention ever made was the internet.
You can find a lot of information in the internet.
I use the internet to do my homework.
I also use it to email my friends or post my pictures.

ON YOUR OWN

WORD BOX

1 another

2 communication

3 nearer

4 greatest

5 post

해답
1. another 또 다른
2. communication 의사소통
3. nearer 더욱 가까운
4. greatest 가장 큰
5. post 두다

Key Expression Practice

LISTEN TO THE CD AND FILL IN THE BLANK.

1. It will also be handy because you can ________________ .

2. They ___________ have to travel for a long time.

3. It made people _________ and _________ .

4. You can find __________________ in the internet.

LISTEN TO THE CD AND WRITE THE SENTENCE.

1. --

2. --

3. --

4. --

TOPIC 27

GRADES

WORD LEVEL

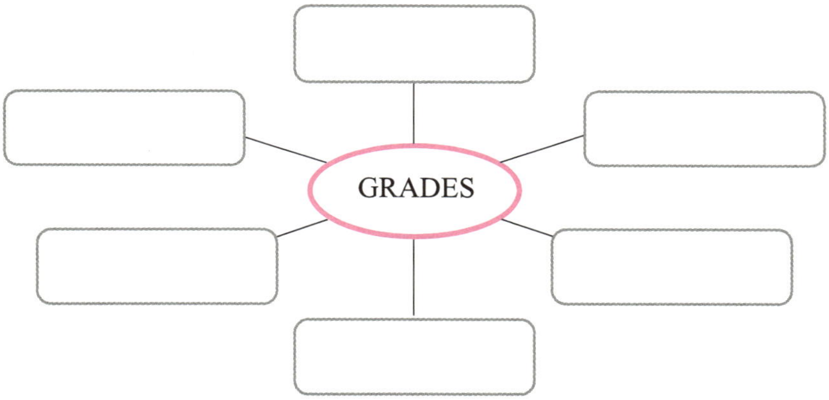

PHRASE LEVEL

1. ______________________ 2. ______________________

3. ______________________ 4. ______________________

SENTENCE LEVEL

1. ____

2. ____

1 Question

Q What is the highest grade you have received? What subject was it?

WORD BOX

1 receive

2 be proud of

3 perfect

4 highest score

5 expect

해답
1. receive 받다
2. be proud of ~을 자랑스러워하다
3. perfect 완전한
4. highest score 가장 높은 점수
5. expect 기대하다

POSSIBLE ANSWER I

The highest grade that I have received was a 99.
I got it when I passed my English exams.
My score was the highest in the class.
My parents were very proud of me.

POSSIBLE ANSWER II

I got a score of 100 on my math exam.
It was a perfect score.
I really studied hard just to pass the test.
I didn't expect that I would get the highest score.

ON YOUR OWN

2 Question

Q What is the lowest grade that you have ever received? What subject was it?

POSSIBLE ANSWER I

The lowest grade that I got was an 80.
We had a practical test in PE.
I am not an athletic person.
So I did not get a good grade.

POSSIBLE ANSWER II

I got a 75 on my last math exam.
It was a surprise test.
I was not prepared and I did not study my lesson.
That's why I got a bad grade.

ON YOUR OWN

WORD BOX

1 lowest

2 grade

3 athletic person

4 surprise test

5 prepared

해답

1. lowest 가장 낮은
2. grade 등급, 점수
3. athletic person 운동을 잘하는 사람
4. surprise test 깜짝 시험
5. prepared 준비된

Key Expression Practice

LISTEN TO THE CD AND FILL IN THE BLANK.

1. ________________ that I have received was a 99.

2. I really studied hard just to ______________ .

3. So I did not ________________ .

4. I ________________ and I did not study my lesson.

LISTEN TO THE CD AND WRITE THE SENTENCE.

1. --

2. --

3. --

4. --

TOPIC 28

HOUSEHOLD CHORES

WORD LEVEL

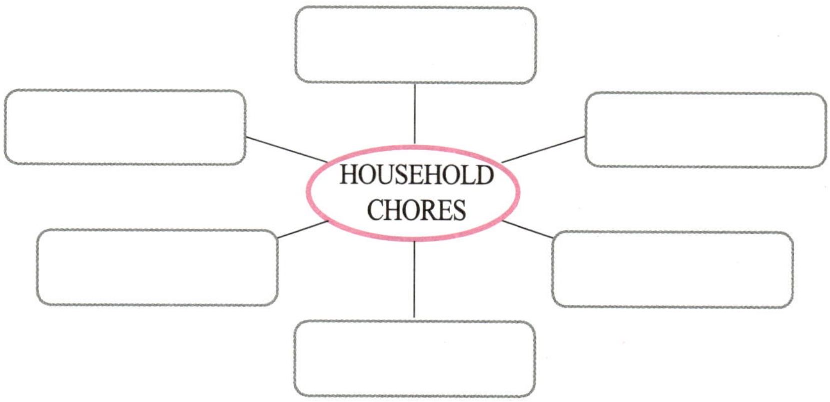

PHRASE LEVEL

1. ______________________ 2. ______________________

3. ______________________ 4. ______________________

SENTENCE LEVEL

1. ____

2. ____

1 Question

Q Do you think children should be required to help in the house? Why or why not?

POSSIBLE ANSWER I

I think children should help in the house.
It teaches them how to manage things.
It will help them when they live on their own.
I help in the house with washing dishes or cleaning my room.

POSSIBLE ANSWER II

I don't think children should help in the house.
They should concentrate on their studying.
My mom doesn't make me help her with household chores.
I just study in my room.

WORD BOX

1. on their own
2. wash dishes
3. concentrate on
4. household chores
5. manage

해답

1. on their own 자기들 스스로
2. wash dishes 설거지를 하다
3. concentrate on 집중하다
4. household chores 집안 일
5. manage 처리하다

ON YOUR OWN

2 Question

Q Do you help in the house? What household chores can you do?

POSSIBLE ANSWER I

Yes, I help in our house.
I clean my room and make the bed everyday.
I also help my father wash the car.
Sometimes, I vacuum the house, too.

POSSIBLE ANSWER II

Yes, I help in the house.
My mom asks me to help her when she is cooking.
She teaches me how to cook.
Sometimes, I cook for my family.

ON YOUR OWN

WORD BOX

1. make the bed
2. everyday
3. wash the car
4. vacuum
5. sometimes

해답

1. make the bed 잠자리를 정리하다
2. everyday 매일
3. wash the car 세차하다
4. vacuum 진공청소하다
5. sometimes 때때로

Key Expression Practice

LISTEN TO THE CD AND FILL IN THE BLANK.

1. It teaches them ______________ things.
2. They should ______________ their studying.
3. I clean my room and ______________ everyday.
4. My mom asks me to help her ______________ .

LISTEN TO THE CD AND WRITE THE SENTENCE.

1. --
2. --
3. --
4. --

TOPIC 29

HABITS

WORD LEVEL

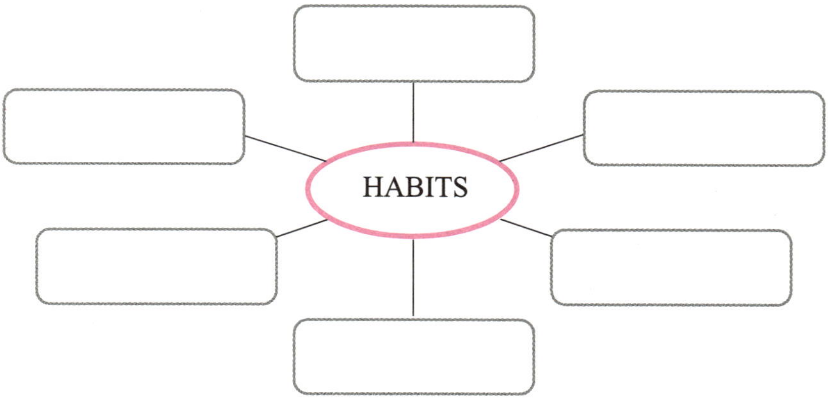

PHRASE LEVEL

1. ______________________ 2. ______________________

3. ______________________ 4. ______________________

SENTENCE LEVEL

1. ____

2. ____

1 Question

Q What is your worst habit that you want to change?

WORD BOX

1. nail biting
2. nervous
3. bored
4. particular
5. definitely

POSSIBLE ANSWER I

I think the worst habit that I have is nail biting.
I bite my nails when I am nervous.
I bite my nails when I am bored, too.
I want to change it because I know it is not a good habit.
My mom usually scolds me when she notices it.

POSSIBLE ANSWER II

I don't think I have any particular bad habit.
But if I have one, I would definitely change it.
People with bad habits should try to change the bad habit.
They will become a better person.

ON YOUR OWN

해답

1. nail biting 손톱 물어뜯기
2. nervous 불안해하는
3. bored 지루한
4. particular 특별한
5. definitely 틀림없이

2 Question

Q Tell us one bad habit that you removed.

POSSIBLE ANSWER I

I used to snore when sleeping.
So I couldn't sleep with other family members in one room.
One day a friend of mine told me one method.
It worked and the snoring stopped.

POSSIBLE ANSWER II

I blinked when I talked.
It happened so frequently.
People thought that I had a serious problem with my eyes.
I went to see a doctor.
He said, "It's just a habit."
After that, I tried not to blink.
And surprisingly it worked successfully.

ON YOUR OWN

WORD BOX

1 snore

2 method

3 blink

4 frequently

5 serious

해답

1. snore 코를 골다
2. method 방법
3. blink 깜박거리다
4. frequently 자주
5. serious 심각한

Key Expression Practice

LISTEN TO THE CD AND FILL IN THE BLANK.

1. My mom usually scolds me ________________ .

2. People with bad habits should try to ________________ .

3. I ________________ when sleeping.

4. I blinked ________________ .

LISTEN TO THE CD AND WRITE THE SENTENCE.

1. ____

2. ____

3. ____

4. ____

TOPIC 30

HEALTH

WORD LEVEL

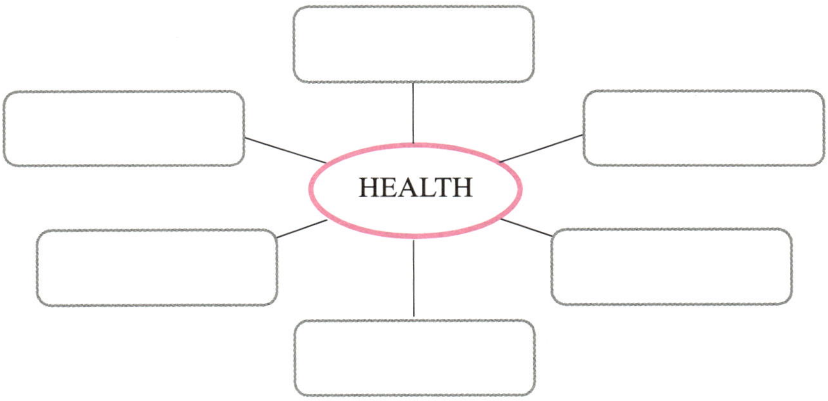

PHRASE LEVEL

1.

2.

3.

4.

SENTENCE LEVEL

1.

2.

1 Question

Q What should you do to keep healthy?

WORD BOX

1 nutritious

2 exercise

3 organic

4 surely

5 fit

POSSIBLE ANSWER I

I think eating healthy food and vegetables will make our bodies healthy.
I like eating vegetables and fruits.
Fruits and vegetables are very nutritious and delicious.
I also eat organic food.

POSSIBLE ANSWER II

I think we have to exercise to keep our bodies healthy.
My father loves jogging.
I like going with him, too.
We usually jog in the morning.
It is a very good exercise and it surely keeps us fit and healthy.

ON YOUR OWN

해답
1. nutritious 영양가 있는
2. exercise 운동
3. organic 유기농의
4. surely 틀림없이
5. fit 건강한

2 Question

Q Do you like going to the doctor for a check-up? Why?

POSSIBLE ANSWER I

I like going to the doctor for a check up.
I want to know if I am sick.
What if I have any diseases?
My mom usually takes me to the doctor every 6 months for a check-up.

POSSIBLE ANSWER II

I don't like going to the doctor.
I am scared of getting a shot.
I remember having a shot when I was sick.
It was so painful.
I would never go to a doctor unless it is really necessary.

ON YOUR OWN

WORD BOX

1. necessary
2. disease
3. be scared of
4. have/get a shot
5. painful

해답
1. necessary 필요한
2. disease 질병
3. be scared of 무서워하다
4. have/get a shot 주사를 맞다
5. painful 고통스러운

Key Expression Practice

LISTEN TO THE CD AND FILL IN THE BLANK.

1. Fruits and vegetables are very ____________ and ____________ .

2. It is a very good exercise and it surely keeps us _____ and _________ .

3. I like going to the doctor _______________ .

4. I remember _______________ when I was sick.

LISTEN TO THE CD AND WRITE THE SENTENCE.

1. --

2. --

3. --

4. --

TOPIC 31

HOMEWORK

WORD LEVEL

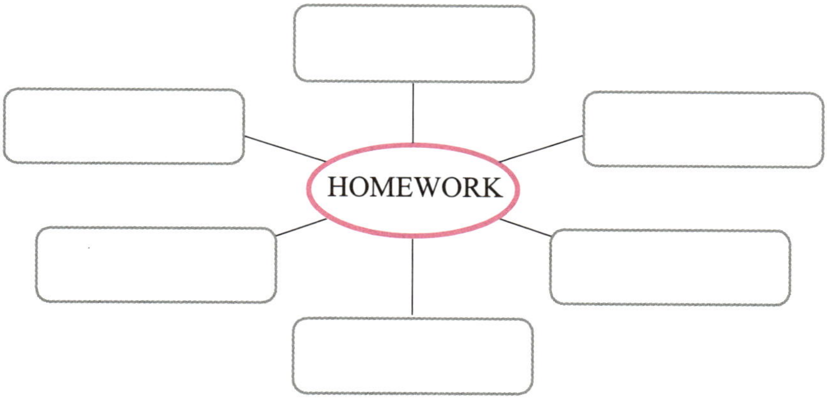

PHRASE LEVEL

1. ______________________ 2. ______________________

3. ______________________ 4. ______________________

SENTENCE LEVEL

1. ____

2. ____

1 Question

Q What is the most difficult homework that you have ever done?

WORD BOX

1. difficult
2. write an essay
3. understand
4. thick
5. biography

해답
1. difficult 어려운
2. write an essay 글을 쓰다
3. understand 이해하다
4. thick 두꺼운
5. biography 전기

POSSIBLE ANSWER I

The most difficult homework I have ever done was writing a book report.
We were asked to read a book and write an essay.
The book was very hard to understand.
It was also very thick so I had to spend a lot of time to finish it.

POSSIBLE ANSWER II

Our history homework was the hardest one I have ever had before.
Our teacher told us to read something about famous people in history.
We were asked to write a biography.
It was difficult because we had to write it all in English.

ON YOUR OWN

2 Question

Q Have you ever done a group project before? How was your experience?

POSSIBLE ANSWER I

Yes, we had a group project before.
We made a model of the solar system.
All of my group mates participated.
We all did our part and we finished the project early.

POSSIBLE ANSWER II

Yes, we did a group project once.
We made a plan to take a tour in the United States.
My group mates did not participate well.
We were not able to finish the project in time.

ON YOUR OWN

WORD BOX

1 solar system

2 mate

3 participate

4 take a tour

5 be able to

해답

1. solar system 태양계
2. mate 친구
3. participate 참석하다
4. take a tour 여행을 하다
5. be able to 할 수 있다

Key Expression Practice

LISTEN TO THE CD AND FILL IN THE BLANK.

1. We ______________________ and write an essay.

2. It was difficult because we had to ____________ in English.

3. We all ____________ and we finished the project early.

4. We were not able to ________________ in time.

LISTEN TO THE CD AND WRITE THE SENTENCE.

1. --

2. --

3. --

4. --

TOPIC 32

LANGUAGE

WORD LEVEL

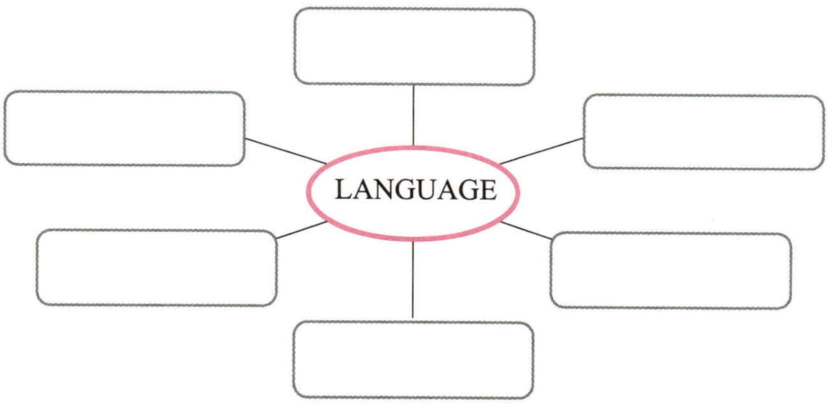

PHRASE LEVEL

1. ______________________ 2. ______________________

3. ______________________ 4. ______________________

SENTENCE LEVEL

1. ____

2. ____

1 Question

Q If you could learn one language, what would it be and why?

WORD BOX

1. be good at
2. almost
3. fluent
4. learn
5. powerful

POSSIBLE ANSWER I

I want to be very good at speaking English.
English is spoken by almost everyone in the world.
I want to study in the United States.
So I have to be a very fluent English speaker.

POSSIBLE ANSWER II

I want to learn how to speak Chinese.
A lot of people speak Chinese nowadays.
I think China will be a powerful country soon.
So I need to learn Chinese so I can talk with them.

ON YOUR OWN

해답

1. be good at ~를 잘하다
2. almost 거의
3. fluent 유창한
4. learn 배우다
5. powerful 힘 있는

2 Question

Q What do you think is the most difficult language to learn? Why?

POSSIBLE ANSWER I

I think the most difficult language to learn is French.
I've heard some people speaking French.
I find it hard to understand.
It sounds very difficult to me.

POSSIBLE ANSWER II

I think it is hard to learn Russian.
A Russian teacher once visited our school.
Their language sounded like a totally different language.
I don't think I will be able to learn it.

ON YOUR OWN

WORD BOX

1. French
2. Russian
3. totally
4. sound like
5. visit

해답

1. French 불어
2. Russian 러시아어
3. totally 전적으로
4. sound like ~처럼 들리다
5. visit 방문하다

Key Expression Practice

LISTEN TO THE CD AND FILL IN THE BLANK.

1. __________ by almost everyone in the world.

2. So I __________ Chinese so I can talk with them.

3. I think __________ language to learn is French.

4. Their language __________ a totally different language.

LISTEN TO THE CD AND WRITE THE SENTENCE.

1. --

2. --

3. --

4. --

TOPIC 33

LIBRARY

WORD LEVEL

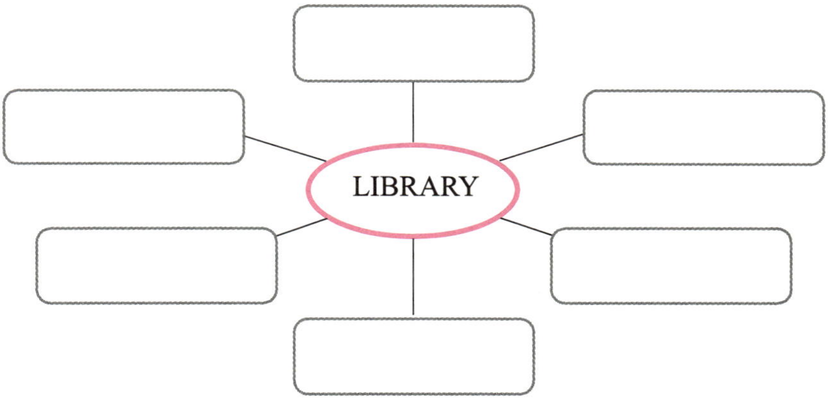

PHRASE LEVEL

1. ______________________ 2. ______________________

3. ______________________ 4. ______________________

SENTENCE LEVEL

1. ____

2. ____

1 Question

Q If you can borrow only one book from the library now, what would you choose?

WORD BOX

1. borrow
2. easy
3. would like to
4. choose
5. for one night

POSSIBLE ANSWER I

If I could, I would borrow an essay book.
Essay books are easy to read.
By reading them, I can feel relaxed.
When you can't sleep well, it's also good to read an essay.

POSSIBLE ANSWER II

I would like to choose a novel.
I can't read many novels because of my school work.
So I want to read a novel if I have to borrow only one book.
I think I can read the whole book in one night.

ON YOUR OWN

해답

1. borrow 빌리다
2. easy 쉬운
3. would like to ~하고 싶다
4. choose 고르다
5. for one night 하룻 밤 동안

2 Question

Q Which do you like better, reading at home or in the library?

POSSIBLE ANSWER I

No doubt, I like reading at home better than in the library.
I don't like people around me when I'm reading.
I prefer a silent place.
So I will definitely choose my room for reading.

POSSIBLE ANSWER II

I think libraries exist for people to come and read books.
There are many books and other materials that I can look at anytime.
And I can also enjoy many other facilities.
If I'm hungry, I can use the cafeteria down at the basement.
Libraries are my best friend.

ON YOUR OWN

WORD BOX

1. no doubt
2. silent
3. exist
4. material
5. basement

해답
1. no doubt 의심할 여지없이
2. silent 조용한
3. exist 존재하다
4. material 자료
5. basement 지하실

Key Expression Practice

LISTEN TO THE CD AND FILL IN THE BLANK.

1. By reading them, I can ______________ .

2. So I want to read a novel ____________________ only one book.

3. So I will ____________________ my room for reading.

4. I think ________________ for people to come and read books.

LISTEN TO THE CD AND WRITE THE SENTENCE.

1. --

2. --

3. --

4. --

TOPIC 34

MEALS

WORD LEVEL

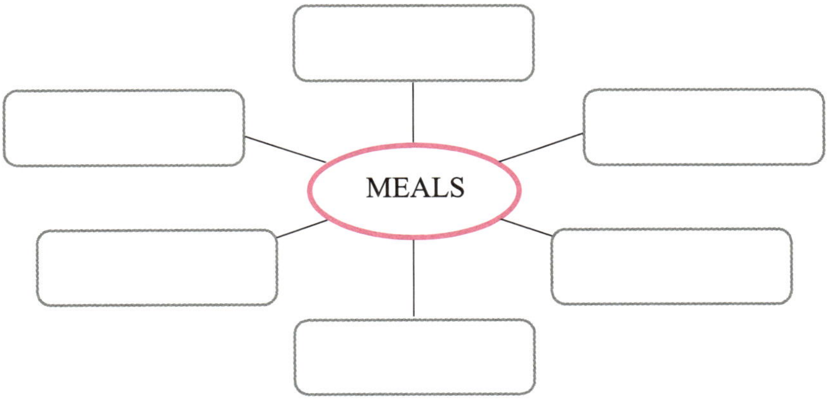

PHRASE LEVEL

1. ____________________ 2. ____________________

3. ____________________ 4. ____________________

SENTENCE LEVEL

1. ____

2. ____

1 Question

Q What did you eat for breakfast today?

WORD BOX

1 a glass of

2 peanut butter

3 cafeteria

4 available

5 depend on

해답

1. a glass of 한잔의
2. peanut butter 땅콩버터
3. cafeteria 구내식당
4. available 사용가능한
5. depend on ~에 달려있다

POSSIBLE ANSWER I

I had toast and milk for breakfast today.
I like putting peanut butter and jelly on my toast.
I also drank a glass of milk.
I also ate some fruits.

POSSIBLE ANSWER II

I usually don't eat breakfast.
I just buy food in the school cafeteria.
It depends on what foods are available on the menu.
I bought a sandwich and juice today.

ON YOUR OWN

2 Question

Q What is the most important meal of the day for you? Why?

POSSIBLE ANSWER I

I think the most important meal of the day is breakfast.
I eat a lot at breakfast.
It helps me to be strong throughout the day.
I don't go hungry easily if I eat breakfast.
When I don't have my breakfast, I can hardly concentrate on my studies.

POSSIBLE ANSWER II

I think the most important meal of the day is dinner.
It is also the most delicious.
My mom prepares a lot of special and delicious dishes for dinner.
If I don't eat dinner, I can hardly go to sleep.

ON YOUR OWN

WORD BOX

1. can hardly
2. concentrate on
3. prepare
4. special
5. go to sleep

해답

1. can hardly 거의 ~할 수 없다
2. concentrate on 집중하다
3. prepare 준비하다
4. special 특별한
5. go to sleep 잠을 자다

Key Expression Practice

LISTEN TO THE CD AND FILL IN THE BLANK.

1. I had ____________________ for breakfast today.

2. It ________________ what foods are available on the menu.

3. I don't ____________________ if I eat breakfast.

4. If I don't eat dinner, I _______________ go to sleep.

LISTEN TO THE CD AND WRITE THE SENTENCE.

1. --

2. --

3. --

4. --

TOPIC 35

MEDICINES

WORD LEVEL

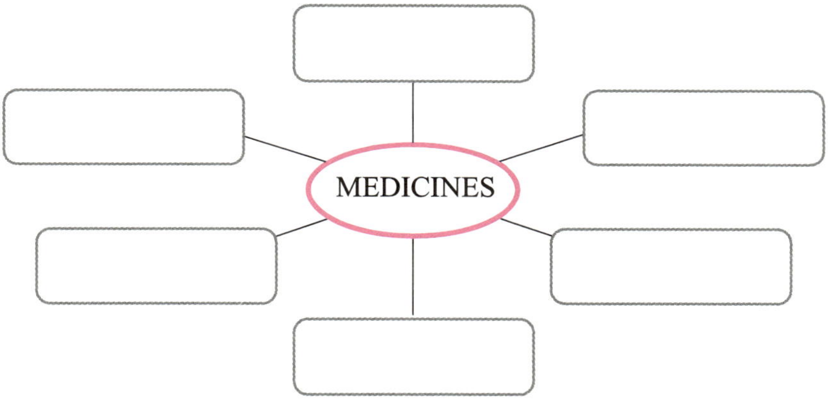

PHRASE LEVEL

1.

2.

3.

4.

SENTENCE LEVEL

1.

2.

1 Question

Q Do you take medicine when you are sick?

WORD BOX

1. of course
2. take medicines
3. rest
4. chicken soup
5. sweat

POSSIBLE ANSWER I

Of course, I take medicines when I am sick.
My mom gives me medicine so I can get well.
I also stay in bed and get a lot of rest.
I believe that medicines help me to get well soon.

POSSIBLE ANSWER II

No, I don't take medicines even though I am sick.
I just get enough rest and sleep.
Mom cooks me a hot chicken soup.
I sweat and I feel much better when I wake up.
I also drink a lot of fruit juice or hot teas.

ON YOUR OWN

해답

1. of course 물론
2. take medicines 약을 먹다
3. rest 쉬다
4. chicken soup 닭 죽
5. sweat 땀을 흘리다

2 Question

Q What do you prefer home remedies or medicines?

POSSIBLE ANSWER I

I know that home remedies are better than medicine.
I don't like cough syrups when I have a cough.
It tastes bitter.
My mom makes some home remedies.
Taking home remedies has no side effects.

POSSIBLE ANSWER II

In order to get well, I think I should take some medicines.
If it is serious, I had better get injections.
Home remedies are good but medicines are much better.
Some people get even worse not by taking medicine.
Medicines are proven in the tests.

ON YOUR OWN

WORD BOX

1. home remedy
2. injection
3. taste bitter
4. side effect
5. prove

정답

1. home remedy 가정(민간)요법
2. injection 주사
3. taste bitter 맛이 쓰다
4. side effect 부작용
5. prove 증명하다

Key Expression Practice

LISTEN TO THE CD AND FILL IN THE BLANK.

1. I believe that medicines help me to ________________ .

2. I sweat and I ________________ when I wake up.

3. Taking home remedies have no ______________ .

4. ________________ , I had better get injections.

LISTEN TO THE CD AND WRITE THE SENTENCE.

1. --

2. --

3. --

4. --

TOPIC 36

MONEY

WORD LEVEL

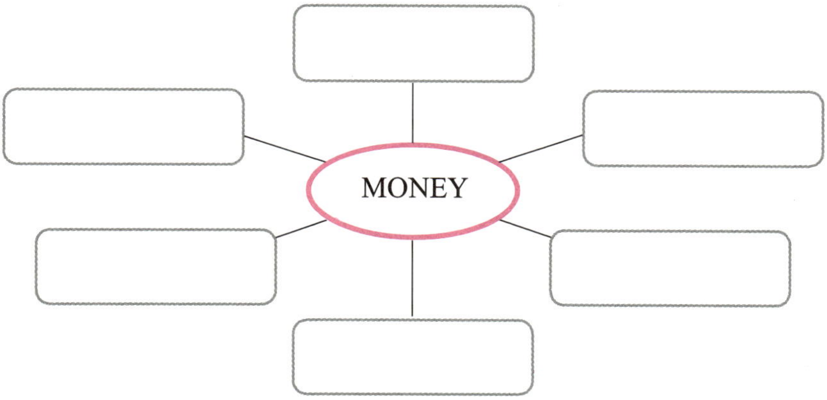

PHRASE LEVEL

1. ______________________ 2. ______________________

3. ______________________ 4. ______________________

SENTENCE LEVEL

1. ____

2. ____

1 Question

Q If you are saving money now, what are you planning to buy?

WORD BOX

1. top secret
2. present
3. surprised
4. allowance
5. a rainy day

POSSIBLE ANSWER I

Well, it's top secret.
I am saving some money for a special present.
I plan to buy my mother a present.
Her 46th birthday is coming soon.
I want to make her surprised.

POSSIBLE ANSWER II

I am saving money now but I don't plan to buy anything.
I just want to save my allowance for the future.
I have a big piggy bank at home.
I always prepare for a rainy day.

ON YOUR OWN

해답

1. top secret 일급 비밀
2. present 선물
3. surprised 놀란
4. allowance 용돈
5. a rainy day 궂은(가난한) 날

2 Question

Q What do you spend most of your money on?

POSSIBLE ANSWER I

I usually spend my money on books.
Books are my best friend.
I get most of my information from books.
Without books, I am nothing.
So I invest my money in books.
When I have money, I buy books.

POSSIBLE ANSWER II

I spend my money on buying cool gadgets.
I just bought a new head set.
I also bought a new lap top computer recently.
Sometimes I buy video games and play them on my computer.
Foods disappear but gadgets remain next to me for a long time.

ON YOUR OWN

WORD BOX

1 information

2 invest

3 recently

4 remain

5 disappear

해답
1. information 정보
2. invest 투자하다
3. recently 최근에
4. remain 남다
5. disappear 사라지다

Key Expression Practice

LISTEN TO THE CD AND FILL IN THE BLANK.

1. I am saving some money ______________ .

2. I am saving money now but I don't ________ buy anything.

3. So I ________ my money ______ books.

4. Foods disappear but gadgets remain ______________ .

LISTEN TO THE CD AND WRITE THE SENTENCE.

1. --

2. --

3. --

4. --

TOPIC 37

MOVIES

WORD LEVEL

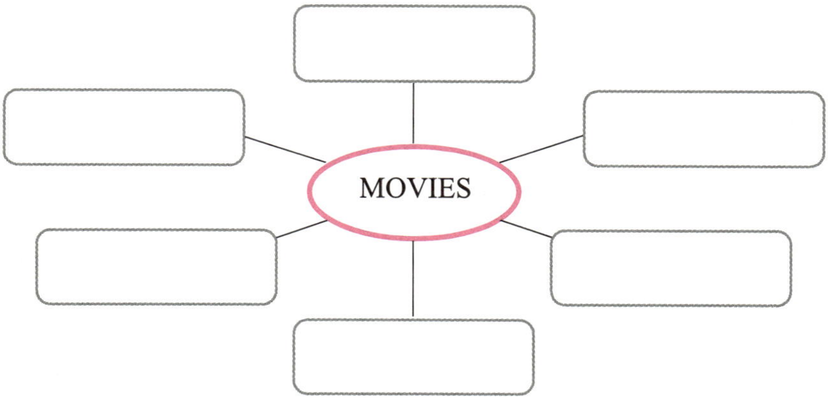

PHRASE LEVEL

1. ______________________ 2. ______________________

3. ______________________ 4. ______________________

SENTENCE LEVEL

1. ____

2. ____

1 Question

Q What is your all-time favorite movie?

WORD BOX

1. travel
2. elf
3. touching
4. impressed
5. mentally retarded

해답
1. travel 여행하다
2. elf 꼬마 요정
3. touching 감동적인
4. impressed 인상받은
5. mentally retarded 정신지체인

POSSIBLE ANSWER I

My all-time favorite movie is the Lord of the Rings.
I like watching it because it is very cool and exciting.
The movie lets you travel into another world.
I would like to be an elf just like the ones in the movie.

POSSIBLE ANSWER II

My all-time favorite movie is I AM SAM.
It is a very touching story.
I got impressed and I even cried when I first watched it.
It's a movie about a mentally retarded father and his daughter.

ON YOUR OWN

2 Question

Q Do you think the ticket price for movies is reasonable?

POSSIBLE ANSWER I

Absolutely not.
It's too expensive. It's a rip-off.
I don't understand why it should be that expensive.
The film makers pay the actors too much, I think.
They should cut back on the film making price.
That's why people download movies illegally.

POSSIBLE ANSWER II

I think it is reasonable.
A friend of mine whose father is a movie director told me so.
Think about all the expenses!
And they make films for money, they should earn money.
In addition, not all movies are successful.

ON YOUR OWN

WORD BOX

1. expensive
2. rip-off
3. cut down
4. illegally
5. reasonable

해답
1. expensive 비싼
2. rip-off 바가지
3. cut down 줄이다
4. illegally 불법적으로
5. reasonable 합리적인

Key Expression Practice

LISTEN TO THE CD AND FILL IN THE BLANK.

1. The movie ________________ into another world.

2. I ________________ and I even cried when I first watched it.

3. ______________ people download movies illegally.

4. ______________ , not all movies are successful.

LISTEN TO THE CD AND WRITE THE SENTENCE.

1. --

2. --

3. --

4. --

TOPIC 38

PARENTS

WORD LEVEL

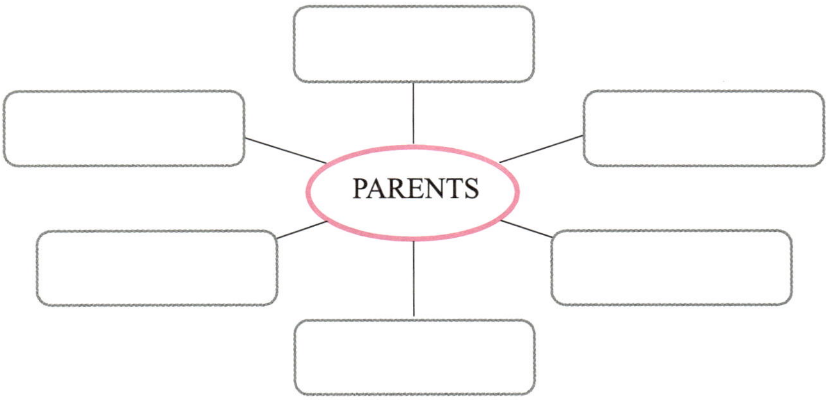

PHRASE LEVEL

1. ______________________ 2. ______________________

3. ______________________ 4. ______________________

SENTENCE LEVEL

1. ____

2. ____

1 Question

Q When you grow up, what type of parent would you like to become?

POSSIBLE ANSWER I

Well, it's hard to say.
I would like to be a father who cares for children.
And I will always be understanding and caring.
If my children say something, I will listen carefully to them.

POSSIBLE ANSWER II

I would like to become a role model to my son or daughter.
They need a role model who guides them.
I will not teach them, but do many things together.
I will travel, shop, play, read, work, and study with them.
I will always put my children in the first place.

WORD BOX

1. understanding
2. caring
3. carefully
4. role model
5. in the first place

해답

1. understanding 이해심이 있는
2. caring 돌보는
3. carefully 주의 깊게
4. role model 역할 모델
5. in the first place 무엇보다도(첫 위치에)

ON YOUR OWN

2 Question

Q What one thing would you like to change about your parents?

POSSIBLE ANSWER I

My parents are so nice that there's a little that I want them to change.
But here is one thing that I would like to mention.
My father smokes and often drinks too much.
So I want him to stop smoking and drinking too much.
If he doesn't smoke and drink, he will be a perfect man!

POSSIBLE ANSWER II

Well, I want to talk about my mother.
She is kind, gentle, and understanding.
But she is very talkative.
She always keeps talking on the phone.
She really loves talking with others on the phone.
Mom, please!!

ON YOUR OWN

WORD BOX

1 few

2 mention

3 perfect

4 talkative

5 on the phone

해답
1. few 거의 없는
2. mention 언급하다
3. perfect 완벽한
4. talkative 말이 많은
5. on the phone 전화상

Key Expression Practice

LISTEN TO THE CD AND FILL IN THE BLANK.

1. And I will always be __________ and __________ .
2. I will always put my children __________ .
3. If he doesn't smoke and drink, he will be __________!
4. She is __________ and __________ .

LISTEN TO THE CD AND WRITE THE SENTENCE.

1. --
2. --
3. --
4. --

TOPIC 39

PETS

WORD LEVEL

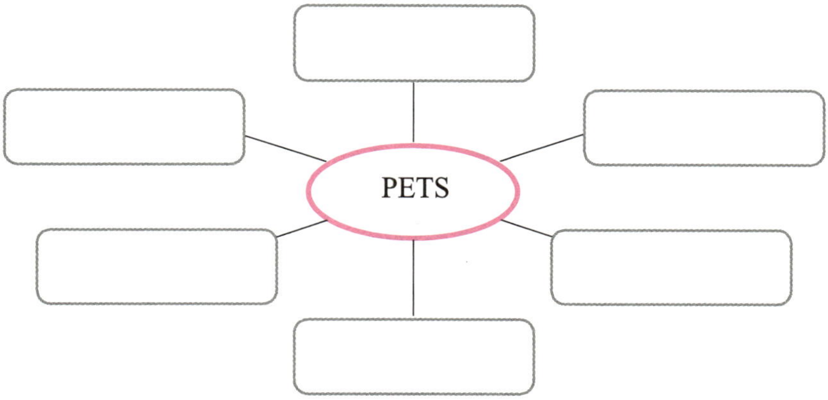

PHRASE LEVEL

1.

2.

3.

4.

SENTENCE LEVEL

1.

2.

1 Question

Q Which animal do you prefer for a pet, a cat or a dog? Why?

WORD BOX

1. protect
2. creature
3. run around
4. make a mess
5. calm

POSSIBLE ANSWER I

I prefer a dog than a cat.
Dogs are man's best friend, I believe.
Sometimes they save man's life.
I like running with my dog in the park.
My dog can also protect my family and guard the house.

POSSIBLE ANSWER II

I prefer to have a cat than a dog.
Cats are gentle creatures.
They are fun to play with.
Dogs run around and make a mess in the house.
But cats are quiet and calm.

ON YOUR OWN

해답
1. protect 보호하다
2. creature 피조물
3. run around 주변을 뛰어다니다
4. make a mess 소란을 피우다
5. calm 차분한

2 Question

Q If you could have an unusual pet, what would it be and why?

POSSIBLE ANSWER I

If I could have an unusual pet, I would like to have a scorpion.
Many people are scared of scorpions because they have poison.
But they are okay as long as they are not angry.
They eat bugs, insects, and so on.
Next time you can visit my home, you can see some scorpions.

POSSIBLE ANSWER II

I would like to have a chameleon.
I think chameleons are cool pets.
They blend with the surroundings.
They can change their skin color.
What if they come out of the cage and crawl on the floor?

ON YOUR OWN

WORD BOX

1. unusual
2. be scared of
3. and so on
4. blend
5. crawl

정답

1. unusual 평범하지 않은
2. be scared of ~이 무서운
3. and so on 기타 등등
4. blend 섞다
5. crawl 기어다니다

Key Expression Practice

LISTEN TO THE CD AND FILL IN THE BLANK.

1. Sometimes they ______________ .

2. They are ______________ .

3. But they are okay ______________________ .

4. ________ they come out of the cage and crawl on the floor?

LISTEN TO THE CD AND WRITE THE SENTENCE.

1. --

2. --

3. --

4. --

TOPIC 40

PLACES

WORD LEVEL

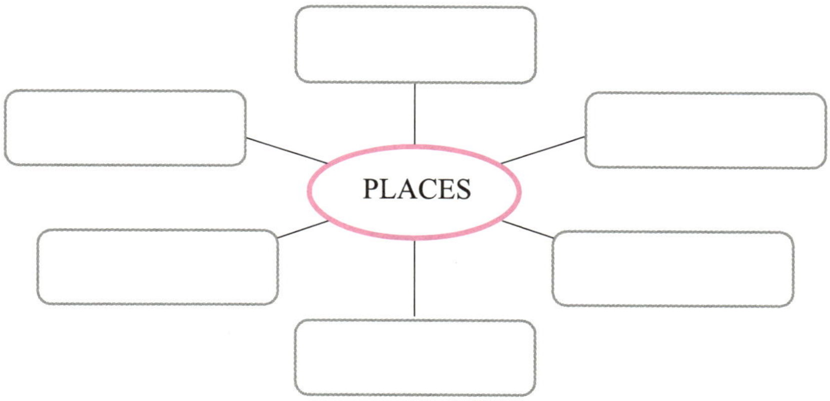

PHRASE LEVEL

1. ______________________ 2. ______________________

3. ______________________ 4. ______________________

SENTENCE LEVEL

1. ____

2. ____

1 Question

Q If you could visit another place, where would you go and why?

WORD BOX

1. go camping
2. only a few
3. in space
4. flag
5. whether

해답

1. go camping 캠핑을 가다
2. only a few 소수의
3. in space 우주에서
4. flag 국기
5. whether -인지 아닌지

POSSIBLE ANSWER I

I would like to go to the Australian Outback.
I want to go camping there with my friends.
I've read a lot about it.
I think it is a very beautiful place.
Would you like to go with me?

POSSIBLE ANSWER II

I would like to go to the moon.
Only a few people have been to the moon.
I want to travel in space in a spaceship.
I will plant my country's flag in the moon.
And I want to take a picture of myself.
I will tell you whether there is a rabbit living there or not.

ON YOUR OWN

2 Question

Q What is your favorite place in your town/city and why?

POSSIBLE ANSWER I

My favorite place is the mall.
I love going to the mall on the weekends.
I can see and buy a lot of things.
My mom is also fond of going shopping with me.

POSSIBLE ANSWER II

My favorite place is our public library.
I usually go there every weekend.
I never eat without reading books.
I borrow books from the library and take them home.
And I never go to bed till I finish reading the entire book.

ON YOUR OWN

WORD BOX

1 be fond of

2 public library

3 every weekend

4 borrow

5 entire

해답

1. be fond of ~를 좋아하다
2. public library 공공 도서관
3. every weekend 매 주말
4. borrow 빌리다
5. entire 전체의

Key Expression Practice

LISTEN TO THE CD AND FILL IN THE BLANK.

1. I want to ______________ there with my friends.
2. ______________ people have been to the moon.
3. My mom ______ also __________ going shopping with me.
4. And I never ____________ till I finish reading the entire book.

LISTEN TO THE CD AND WRITE THE SENTENCE.

1. ____
2. ____
3. ____
4. ____

TOPIC 41

PEOPLE

WORD LEVEL

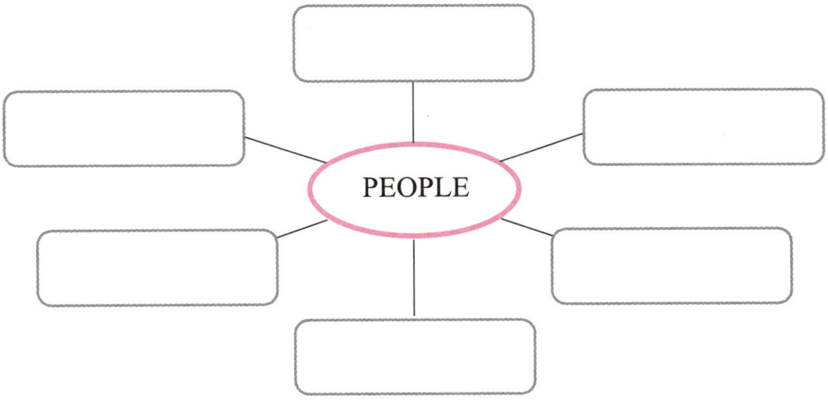

PHRASE LEVEL

1. ______________________ 2. ______________________

3. ______________________ 4. ______________________

SENTENCE LEVEL

1. ____

2. ____

1 Question

Q If you could meet a famous historical person, who would it be and why?

WORD BOX

1. famous
2. intelligent
3. fight
4. violence
5. lose one's temper

POSSIBLE ANSWER I

I want to meet Albert Einstein.
I think he was the most famous scientist who ever lived.
He was a very intelligent man.
My future dream is to be a scientist.
So I would like to learn from him.

POSSIBLE ANSWER II

I want to meet Mahatma Gandhi.
I think he was a very great man.
He fought against the British without using violence.
I lose my temper so easily.
I think I can learn a lot if I meet him.

ON YOUR OWN

해답

1. famous 유명한
2. intelligent 현명한
3. fight 싸움
4. violence 폭력
5. lose one's temper 화를 내다

2 Question

Q Who is the most important person to you and why?

POSSIBLE ANSWER I

The most important person to me is my mother.
I love my mother very much.
She takes good care of me and our family.
She is the best mother in the whole world.
I will marry a woman who is like my mom.

POSSIBLE ANSWER II

The most important person to me is my father.
He is a very good man.
He works hard for our family.
He takes us out when he has free time.
I like taking a walk with him in the park on Sundays.

ON YOUR OWN

WORD BOX

1. take care of
2. in the whole world
3. work hard
4. free time
5. take a walk

해답

1. take care of 돌보다
2. in the whole world 전 세계에서
3. work hard 열심히 일하다.
4. free time 자유시간
5. take a walk 산책을 하다.

Key Expression Practice

LISTEN TO THE CD AND FILL IN THE BLANK.

1. He was a very ______________ man.
2. I ____________________ so easily.
3. She ______________________ me and our family.
4. He ________________ when he has free time.

LISTEN TO THE CD AND WRITE THE SENTENCE.

1. --
2. --
3. --
4. --

TOPIC 42

PERSONAL INFORMATION

WORD LEVEL

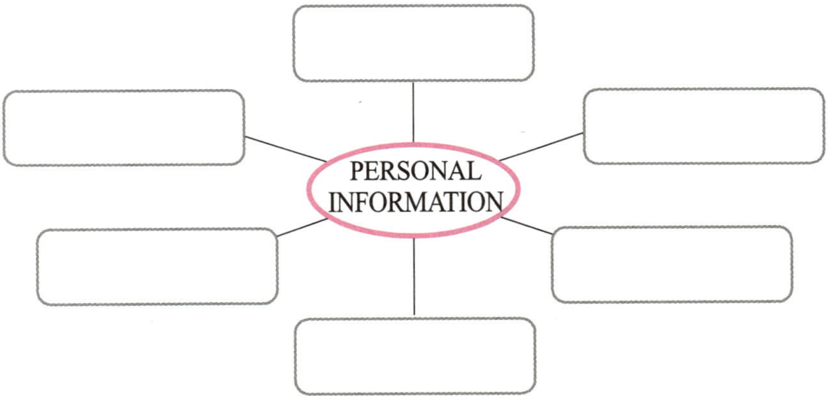

PHRASE LEVEL

1. ______________________ 2. ______________________

3. ______________________ 4. ______________________

SENTENCE LEVEL

1. ____

2. ____

1 Question

Q Tell me something about yourself.

WORD BOX

1. briefly
2. police officer
3. housekeeper
4. the only child
5. engineer

POSSIBLE ANSWER I

Hi, let me briefly introduce myself to you.
There are four of us in my family.
I have a little brother. His name is James.
My father is a police officer.
My mother is a housekeeper.

POSSIBLE ANSWER II

Hello, I would like to talk about myself.
There are three of us in the family.
I am the only child.
My father is an engineer.
My mother is a nurse.

ON YOUR OWN

해답

1. briefly 요약해서
2. police officer 경찰관
3. housekeeper 주부
4. the only child 외동
5. engineer 엔지니어

2 Question

Q Tell me about your daily routine.

POSSIBLE ANSWER I

I think as a student our daily routines are alike.
I get up early morning and get ready for school.
I study at school all morning.
I have lunch at the school cafeteria.
After school, I study English at a private academy.
Coming back home, I wash and eat dinner.
I read some books and do my homework.
And finally I hit the sack.

POSSIBLE ANSWER II

Mine is not different from other students' .
Korean students have almost the same daily routine.

ON YOUR OWN

WORD BOX

1 daily routine

2 alike

3 get ready for

4 private academy

5 hit the sack

해답

1. daily routine 매일 일상
2. alike 같은
3. get ready for ~를 준비하다
4. private academy 사설 학원
5. hit the sack 잠을 자다

Key Expression Practice

LISTEN TO THE CD AND FILL IN THE BLANK.

1. There are ____________ in my family.

2. Hello, I ______________________________ .

3. ____________________ , I wash and eat dinner.

4. Korean students have almost the same ______________ .

LISTEN TO THE CD AND WRITE THE SENTENCE.

1. --

2. --

3. --

4. --

TOPIC 43

SUBJECTS IN SCHOOL

WORD LEVEL

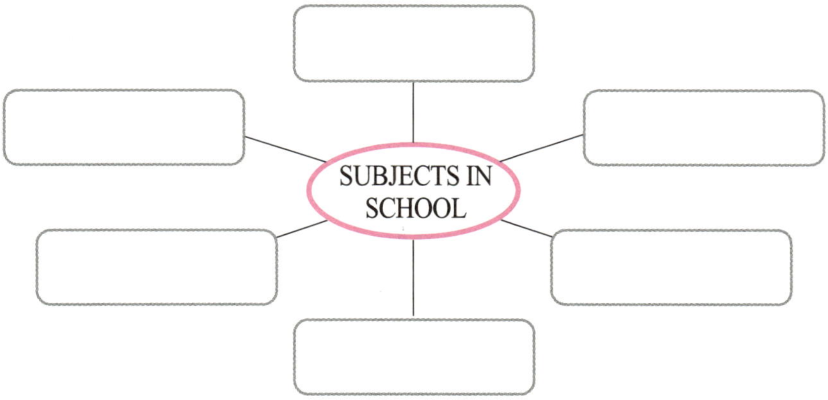

PHRASE LEVEL

1. ______________________ 2. ______________________

3. ______________________ 4. ______________________

SENTENCE LEVEL

1. ____

2. ____

1 Question

Q Which subject is(was) difficult for you? Why?

WORD BOX

1. **solve problems**
2. **passage**
3. **too ~ to ~**
4. **tricky**
5. **mother language**

해답

1. solve problems 문제를 해결하다
2. passage 구문
3. too ~ to- 너무 ~해서 -할 수 없다
4. tricky 어려운
5. mother language 모국어

POSSIBLE ANSWER I

I think math is(was) very difficult.
I am not good at math.
It is because I am not good at numbers.
I find it hard to solve math problems and computations.

POSSIBLE ANSWER II

I think English is(was) very hard.
I cannot understand English grammar.
I am too shy to speak to foreigners.
I find it difficult to read English passages.
English is not my mother language so it's so tricky.

ON YOUR OWN

2 Question

Q What subjects are you good at?

POSSIBLE ANSWER I

I think I am good at English.
I always get good grades in English.
When my teacher asks me, I can answer right away.
I think it is because I started learning English when I was young.

POSSIBLE ANSWER II

I think I am good at science.
I am really into scientific information.
And I always get good grades on my science exams.
Sometimes, I help my classmates with their problems.
My father majored in science, too.
Like father, like son!

ON YOUR OWN

WORD BOX

1 **grade**

2 **right away**

3 **scientific information**

4 **major in**

5 **Like father, like son**

해답
1. grade 학년, 등급
2. right away 지금 당장
3. scientific information 과학 정보
4. major in ~을 전공하다
5. Like father, like son 부전자전

Key Expression Practice

LISTEN TO THE CD AND FILL IN THE BLANK.

1. It is because I ______________________ .

2. English is not my ________________ so it's so tricky.

3. When my teacher asks me, I can answer ____________ .

4. I ______________________ information.

LISTEN TO THE CD AND WRITE THE SENTENCE.

1. --

2. --

3. --

4. --

TOPIC 44

SCHOOL

WORD LEVEL

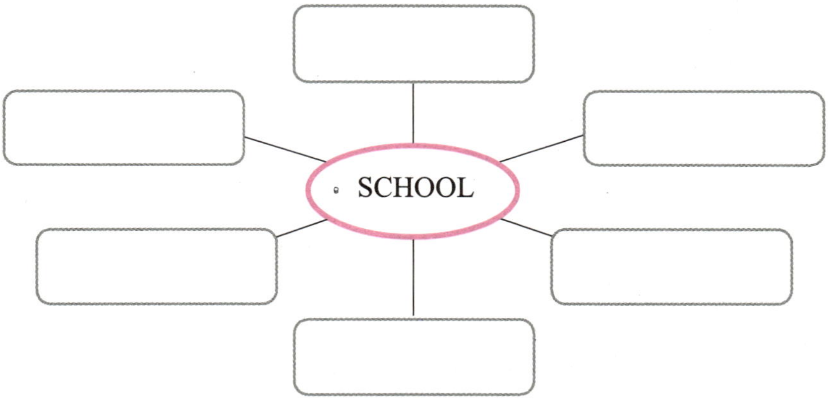

PHRASE LEVEL

1. ________________ 2. ________________

3. ________________ 4. ________________

SENTENCE LEVEL

1. ________________________________

2. ________________________________

1 Question

Q If you were a principal or director of your school, what would you like to do?

WORD BOX

1. gym
2. inside
3. hectic
4. build up
5. less than

POSSIBLE ANSWER I

If I were principal, I will build up a big gym in the school.
Even when it rains, we can play inside.
And I want to buy more books for the library.
I also want to help all the poor students.

POSSIBLE ANSWER II

Well, I will make all the students come to school at 10:00 am.
Coming to school by 8:30 is really difficult.
If I have a hectic morning, the rest of the day is busy.
And one more! The number of students in one class should be less than 25.

ON YOUR OWN

해답

1. gym 체육관
2. inside 안쪽
3. hectic 바쁜
4. build up 짓다, 형성하다
5. less than ~보다 적은

2 Question

Q How was your first day of school this term?

POSSIBLE ANSWER I

The first day of school was exciting and memorable.
I met my new teachers and they were all very nice and friendly to me.
I also met my classmates.
I made a lot of friends this term.

POSSIBLE ANSWER II

The first day of school wasn't good enough to please me.
I was late because the alarm clock didn't ring.
Every one was in class when I entered the room.
On the first day, I was late for class!

ON YOUR OWN

WORD BOX

1. memorable
2. make friends
3. enough
4. please
5. enter

해답

1. memorable 기억에 남는
2. make friends 친구를 사귀다
3. enough 충분한
4. please 즐겁게 하다
5. enter 들어가다

Key Expression Practice

LISTEN TO THE CD AND FILL IN THE BLANK.

1. ____________________, we can play inside.

2. If I have a hectic morning, __________________________.

3. I met my new teachers and they were all very ________ and _________ to me.

4. I was late because __________________ didn't ring.

LISTEN TO THE CD AND WRITE THE SENTENCE.

1. --

2. --

3. --

4. --

TOPIC 45

SLEEP

WORD LEVEL

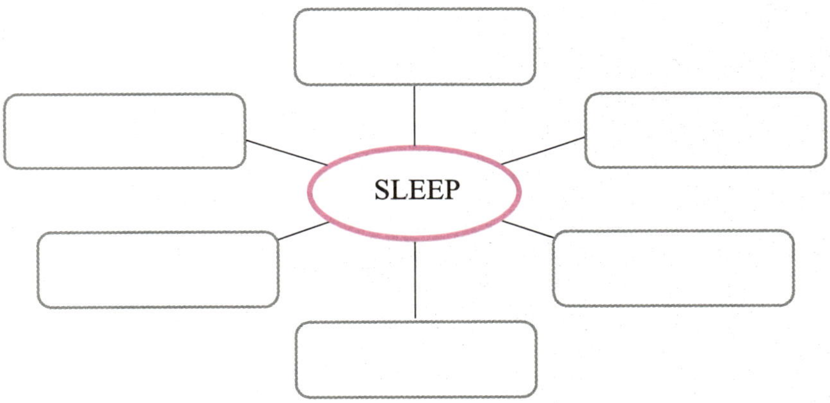

PHRASE LEVEL

1. ______________________ 2. ______________________

3. ______________________ 4. ______________________

SENTENCE LEVEL

1. ____

2. ____

1 Question

Q What sleeping habits do you have?

WORD BOX

1. next to
2. carry
3. sound
4. record
5. be absorbed in

POSSIBLE ANSWER I

I can't sleep well without my teddy bear next to me.
It's a doll that I love so much. And I can't live without it.
I carry it when I sleep out of my house.
It may sound funny but it's true.

POSSIBLE ANSWER II

I talk in English even when I sleep.
I didn't know it but my parents once recorded it.
It is because I am absorbed in English.
I dream in English.

ON YOUR OWN

해답

1. next to ~에 가까운
2. carry 운반하다
3. sound 들리다
4. record 기록하다
5. be absorbed in ~에 몰입하다

2 Question

Q Why is it important to get enough sleep?

POSSIBLE ANSWER I

I think it is important to get enough sleep so that we will not get sick.
If we don't have enough sleep, we feel weak.
We don't have the energy to do our activities.
Sometimes, we are not in the mood to talk or even move.

POSSIBLE ANSWER II

It is important to have enough sleep to concentrate on work.
If we don't sleep well, we cannot work properly.
We cannot think rationally, either.
I think getting enough sleep is good for our health.

ON YOUR OWN

WORD BOX

1. weak
2. energy
3. properly
4. either
5. rationally

해답
1. weak 약한
2. energy 에너지
3. properly 적절하게
4. either 또한(부정문에서)
5. rationally 이성적으로

Key Expression Practice

LISTEN TO THE CD AND FILL IN THE BLANK.

1. I carry it when I ______________ my house.

2. I didn't know it but my parents ________________ .

3. If we don't have enough sleep, we ____________ .

4. I think ____________________ is good for our health.

LISTEN TO THE CD AND WRITE THE SENTENCE.

1. --

2. --

3. --

4. --

TOPIC 46

SHOPPING

WORD LEVEL

PHRASE LEVEL

1. ________________________

2. ________________________

3. ________________________

4. ________________________

SENTENCE LEVEL

1. ________________________

2. ________________________

1 Question

Q What was the last thing you bought when you went shopping?

WORD BOX

1. broken
2. accidentally
3. crushed
4. comfortable
5. a pair of

POSSIBLE ANSWER I

I bought a new watch when I went shopping.
My old watch was broken.
I accidentally sat on it and it was crushed.
My mom bought me a new one and I liked it very much.

POSSIBLE ANSWER II

I bought a new pair of shoes when I went shopping.
My old shoes are worn out.
I use them to play soccer and basketball.
My new shoes are comfortable and fit me well.

ON YOUR OWN

해답

1. broken 고장난
2. accidentally 우연히
3. crushed 부서진
4. comfortable 편안한
5. a pair of 한 쌍의

2 Question

Q What do you consider when you decide to buy something?

POSSIBLE ANSWER I

Price really matters when deciding what to buy.
If I can't afford to buy it, it means nothing to me.
Though the product's quality is good, I can't buy it.
So I always check the price first.

POSSIBLE ANSWER II

I always consider the quality of the product.
If the quality is good, I don't hesitate.
I can use the item for a long time.
It is worthwhile to invest in quality.

ON YOUR OWN

WORD BOX

1. matter
2. it is worthwhile
3. can afford to
4. consider
5. hesitate

해답

1. matter 중요하다
2. it is worthwhile 가치가 있는
3. can afford to
   ~할 능력이 되다
4. consider 고려하다
5. hesitate 망설이다

Key Expression Practice

LISTEN TO THE CD AND FILL IN THE BLANK.

1. I accidentally sat on it and ________________.

2. My new shoes are ______________ and fit me well.

3. If I ________________ buy it, it means nothing to me.

4. If the quality is good, I don't ___________.

LISTEN TO THE CD AND WRITE THE SENTENCE.

1. --

2. --

3. --

4. --

TOPIC 47

SEASONS

WORD LEVEL

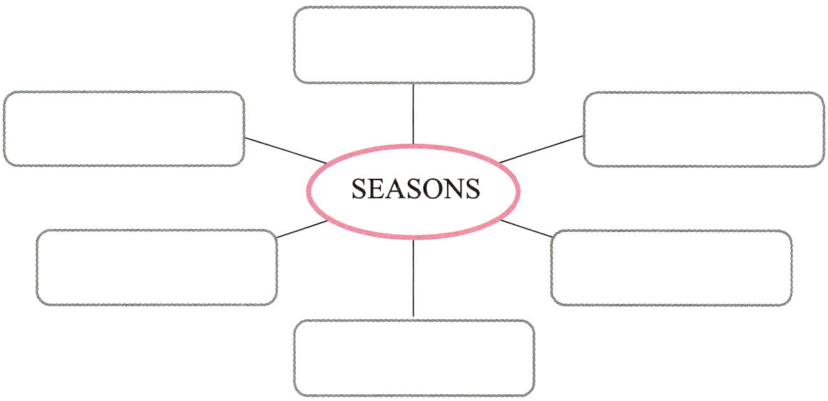

PHRASE LEVEL

1. ______________________ 2. ______________________

3. ______________________ 4. ______________________

SENTENCE LEVEL

1. ____

2. ____

1 Question

Q What is your favorite winter activity?

WORD BOX

1. activity
2. slide down
3. race
4. dry up
5. competition

해답

1. activity 활동
2. slide down 미끄러지다
3. race 경기
4. dry up 마르다
5. competition 경쟁

POSSIBLE ANSWER I

My favorite winter activity is snow boarding.
I like to ride on my snow board and slide down the hill.
I like to race with my friends.
When riding it, I forget my worries.

POSSIBLE ANSWER II

My favorite winter activity is ice hockey.
I play ice hockey with my friends.
We play in the river when it dries up.
Sometimes we also join ice hockey competitions.

ON YOUR OWN

2 Question

Q What did(will) you do last(next) summer?

POSSIBLE ANSWER I

We went on a vacation last summer.
My family went to the beach.
We stayed there for a week.
We swam in the sea and rode a boat.
My father and I caught some fish and ate them.

POSSIBLE ANSWER II

I had swimming lessons last summer.
I learned how to swim and float.
My teacher was very handsome and professional.
My fear of the water has disappeared thanks to his kind coaching.

ON YOUR OWN

WORD BOX

1 vacation

2 professional

3 thanks to

4 fear

5 disappear

해답
1. vacation 방학
2. professional 전문가인
3. thanks to ~의 덕분에
4. fear 두려움
5. disappear 사라지다

Key Expression Practice

LISTEN TO THE CD AND FILL IN THE BLANK.

1. When riding it, I ____________________ .

2. We play in the river __________________ .

3. We swam in the sea and ______________ .

4. My fear of the water has disappeared _____________ his kind coaching.

LISTEN TO THE CD AND WRITE THE SENTENCE.

1. --

2. --

3. --

4. --

TOPIC 48

TELEVISION

WORD LEVEL

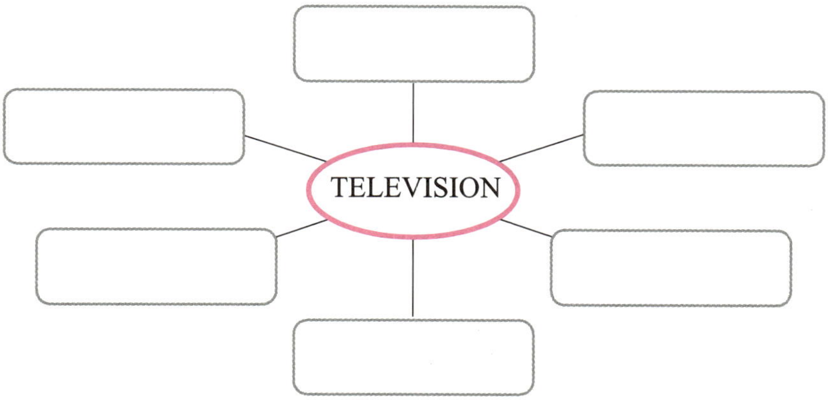

PHRASE LEVEL

1.

2.

3.

4.

SENTENCE LEVEL

1.

2.

1 Question

Q Do you think TV is educational? Why or why not?

WORD BOX

1. educational
2. documentary
3. entertaining
4. kill time
5. commercial

POSSIBLE ANSWER I

Yes, I think TV is educational.
I can watch a lot of good programs and shows.
I can learn a lot of news and information by watching TV.
I especially love watching documentary films.

POSSIBLE ANSWER II

No, I don't think TV is educational.
I think TV is just entertaining.
Watching TV is just good if you want to kill time.
Some TV programs are not adequate for young children.
They are even commercial.

ON YOUR OWN

해답
1. educational 교육적인
2. documentary 다큐멘터리
3. entertaining 오락적인
4. kill time 시간을 보내다
5. commercial 상업적인

2 Question

Q What is your favorite commercial on TV? Why?

POSSIBLE ANSWER I

My favorite commercial is Nike.
I love playing basketball and I like wearing Nike shoes.
The commercial shows a lot of famous athletes.
They all look so cool in their Nike shoes.

POSSIBLE ANSWER II

My favorite commercial is the Samsung Commercial.
I think it is fantastic and attractive.
There are a lot of new cell phone models.
I like the state-of-the-art designs and the features.

ON YOUR OWN

WORD BOX

1. feature
2. athlete
3. attractive
4. fantastic
5. state of the art

해답

1. feature 특징
2. athlete 운동선수
3. attractive 매력적인
4. fantastic 환상적인
5. state of the art : 최첨단의

Key Expression Practice

LISTEN TO THE CD AND FILL IN THE BLANK.

1. I can learn ______________ and ______________ by watching TV.

2. Watching TV is just good if you want to __________ .

3. The commercial shows a lot of ______________ .

4. I like the ______________ designs and the features.

LISTEN TO THE CD AND WRITE THE SENTENCE.

1. --

2. --

3. --

4. --

TOPIC 49

WEEKENDS

WORD LEVEL

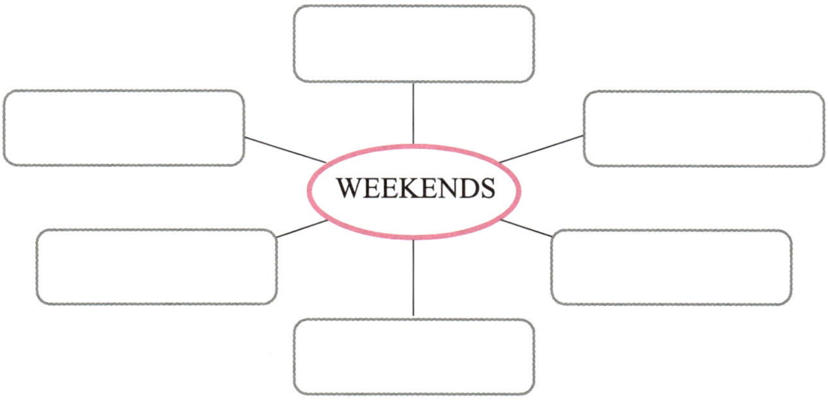

PHRASE LEVEL

1. ______________________ 2. ______________________

3. ______________________ 4. ______________________

SENTENCE LEVEL

1. ____

2. ____

1 Question

Q What is your favorite pastime on weekends? Why?

WORD BOX

1. pastime
2. stay at home
3. make time
4. run errands
5. nothing special

POSSIBLE ANSWER I

My favorite pastime is playing soccer or basketball with my friends.
We play in the park or at the playground.
It has a basketball court and a big soccer field.
Sometimes we go to a Korean dry sauna after the game.

POSSIBLE ANSWER II

I usually just stay at home on weekends.
If my friends can make time, we go shopping together.
Sometimes, I run errands for my mom.
There is nothing special on weekends, in fact.

ON YOUR OWN

해답

1. pastime 여가시간
2. stay at home 집에 머물다
3. make time 시간을 내다
4. run errands 심부름을 하다
5. nothing special 특별한 것이 없는

2 Question

Q Which do you prefer weekdays or weekends? And why?

POSSIBLE ANSWER I

No doubt, I prefer weekends.
I can do many things that I can't do during the weekdays.
I can relax and refresh myself.
I can also do something for my parents and others.

POSSIBLE ANSWER II

It is weekdays that I do most of my work.
So I prefer weekdays. I am a goal-oriented person.
In order to accomplish my goal, I should work.
Weekends come peacefully after hard weekdays.

ON YOUR OWN

WORD BOX

1. refresh
2. during
3. goal-oriented
4. accomplish
5. peacefully

해답

1. refresh 새롭게 하다
2. during ~동안
3. goal-oriented 목표지향적인
4. accomplish 성취하다
5. peacefully 평화롭게

Key Expression Practice

LISTEN TO THE CD AND FILL IN THE BLANK.

1. ______________ we go to Korean dry sauna after the game.

2. If my friends can ______________, we go shopping together.

3. I can do many things that I can't do ______________________.

4. Weekends come _____________ after hard weekdays.

LISTEN TO THE CD AND WRITE THE SENTENCE.

1. --

2. --

3. --

4. --

TOPIC 50

WISHING

WORD LEVEL

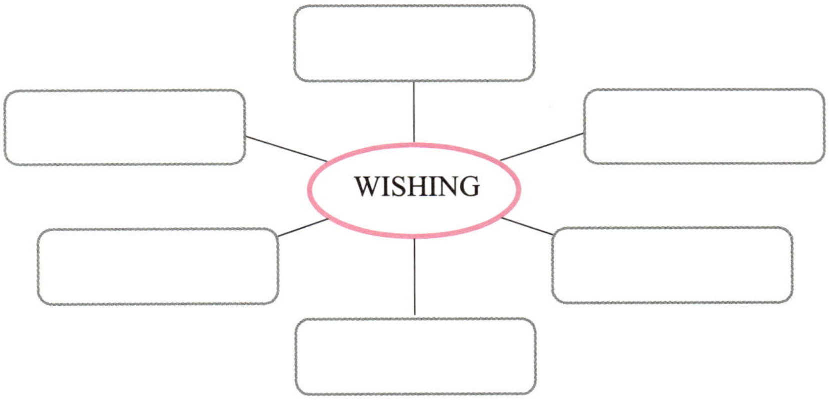

PHRASE LEVEL

1.

2.

3.

4.

SENTENCE LEVEL

1.

2.

1 Question

Q What was your wish on your last birthday?

WORD BOX

1. turtle
2. as ~ as ~
3. palm
4. complain
5. promise

POSSIBLE ANSWER I

I wished for a pet turtle on my last birthday.
My mom bought me two turtles.
I named them each Peeky and Pooky.
My turtles are very cute and they are as big as my palm.

POSSIBLE ANSWER II

I wished for a digital piano on my last birthday.
I can't play the piano in the house because people living downstairs complain.
My parents promised that they would buy me one.
Now I can play the digital piano even after midnight.

ON YOUR OWN

해답
1. turtle 거북이
2. as ~ as ~ -만큼 ~한
3. palm 손바닥
4. complain 불평하다
5. promise 약속하다

2 Question

Q Have you ever wished on a falling star? What did you wish for?

POSSIBLE ANSWER I

Yes, I have seen a falling star before.
I wished for my grandfather's health.
He has been sick in bed for three years.
I just hope that it will come true.
I am sure he will be able to walk with me in the park again.

POSSIBLE ANSWER II

No, I haven't seen a falling star before.
But if I see one, I would like to make a wish.
I would wish to have a very handsome boyfriend.
I would like to live happily with him ever after.

ON YOUR OWN

WORD BOX

1. falling star
2. come true
3. be able to
4. make a wish
5. happily

해답

1. falling star 별똥별
2. come true 실현되다
3. be able to ~할 수 있다
4. make a wish 소원을 빌다
5. happily 행복하게

Key Expression Practice

LISTEN TO THE CD AND FILL IN THE BLANK.

1. My turtles are very cute and they are ____________ .

2. Now I can play the digital piano ____________ .

3. I am sure he will ____________ me in the park again.

4. ____________ have a very handsome boyfriend.

LISTEN TO THE CD AND WRITE THE SENTENCE.

1. --

2. --

3. --

4. --

MEMO

MEMO

BRUSH UP YOUR SPEAKING

2011년 4월 5일 초판 1쇄 인쇄
2011년 4월 8일 초판 1쇄 발행

저자와의 협의하에 인지생략

저 자 : 김 종 춘
발행자 : 김 동 규
발행처 : 교육과학사

경기도 파주시 교하읍 문발리
파주출판문화정보산업단지 514 - 5
전화 (031) 955 - 6956~8 / 팩스 (031) 955 - 6037
Homepage : www.kyoyookbook.co.kr
등록 1970년 5월 18일 제 2-73호

낙장 · 파본은 교환해 드립니다. 정가 14,000원
Printed in Korea. ISBN 978-89-254-0470-7